P9-BYT-949

Teatime Stories for Women

Refreshment and Inspiration to Warm Your Heart

Compiled by

Linda Evans Shepherd

Honor Books
Tulsa, Oklahoma

Unless otherwise indicated, all Scripture quotations are taken from the *Holy Bible, New International Version*®. NIV®. Copyright © 1973, 1978, 1984 by the International Bible Society. Used by permission of Zondervan Publishing House. All rights reserved.

Scripture quotations marked KJV are taken from the *King James Version* of the Bible.

Scripture quotations marked NKJV are taken from *The New King James Version*. Copyright © 1979, 1980, 1982, Thomas Nelson, Inc.

2nd Printing

Teatime Stories for Women:
Refreshment and Inspiration to Warm Your Heart
ISBN 1-56292-594-6
Copyright © 2000 by Linda Evans Shepherd

Published by Honor Books
P.O. Box 55388
Tulsa, Oklahoma 74155

Printed in the United States of America. All rights reserved under International Copyright Law. Contents and/or cover may not be reproduced in whole or in part in any form without the express written consent of the Publisher.

Dedication

Dedicated to Mary Evans and Sharon Shepherd.
Marriage may have made us sisters-in-law, but
friendship made us sisters of the heart. I love you both!

Acknowledgments

I want to give special thanks to Murray Fisher, my agent and dear friend; my personal assistant, Donna Rae Manzanares, who kept me organized; and my wonderful family, who continues to support me in so many ways.

Introduction

I'm so glad you've accepted my invitation to tea. We have so much to talk about. I hope you will enjoy meeting all the special women I've invited.

We'll share laughter and tears, especially when Connie Bertelsen Young tells us her hilarious story, "Do, You Know Where Your Children Are?" Be sure to have your tissues handy for Rachel Hodges' love story, "Sweethearts and Heroes." And wait until you hear Marjorie Evans' account of a tender miracle in "A Davy Crockett Hat for David." These are just a few of the wonderful stories we will enjoy together.

I hope you will be warmed and encouraged as we celebrate the beauty of womanhood with smiles, giggles, and sniffles. I believe that within the pages of this book, you will find friendship and companionship. So come on in, sit down, and have a cup of tea.

Your hostess,

Linda Evans Shepherd

Teatime Stories for Women?

Table of Contents

Living Your Dream

*You must climb upon the bumps of
life in order to reach your dreams.*
Warren W. Wiersbe

Holey, Holey, Holey

Sue Cameron

Command those who are rich in this present world not to be arrogant nor to put their hope in wealth, which is so uncertain, but to put their hope in God, who richly provides us with everything for our enjoyment.

1 Timothy 6:17

Not too many pounds ago, I had three preschoolers. Back then our budget was tight and my jeans were loose. One morning I borrowed a car, loaded up my brood, and headed for Gemco. It was the store with everything: housewares, fabric, clothes, and, way in the back, the lowest-priced groceries in town.

We went in for food, but took a tempting detour through the shoe department, where we ended up parked in front of an array of ladies' socks. I really needed socks. I really needed groceries. I looked down at my neglected feet then up at my three hungry children. No contest. My feet were definitely outnumbered. The choice seemed totally obvious and completely unfair. I knew other people with preschoolers who could afford socks *and* food. I even considered some of those people to be my friends—usually.

I glanced sideways at the other shoppers. Some had new towels in their carts. Others had name-brand shampoo, guaranteed to make your hair smell like an herb garden. *I bet they can afford socks,* I thought. They probably buy the fancy kind with cute little patterns. All I want is plain white cotton.

I reached for the package and examined it. They sure were white. They sure were soft. They sure didn't have holes in the heels.

"Mommy," my two-year-old asked, "you hugging socks?"

The baby squirmed in her front snuggle-carrier.

"Mom," my four-year-old informed me, "you're smashing the baby. Didn't we come in here to get food?"

I looked into the eyes of my trusting children and sighed deeply. Reluctantly I hung the package on the hook. Then I squared my shoulders and pointed the cart toward the grocery section. But before I gave it a forward push, I said a quick prayer. I did not kneel. I did not wail. I did not close my eyes. I just lifted a thought to the One who always hears. *God, I need socks.*

The next day, I answered an unexpected knock on the front door to find Shirley, a lady from church.

"Hi Sue," she said. "My daughter-in-law works at a sporting goods store and has access to some clothes I thought you might be able to use."

"Great!" I said. "I love hand-me-downs."

"Most of these are new," she explained. "Overstocks, discontinued items, or returns."

Shirley brought in four large, black—plastic trash bags.

"Thanks for thinking of me," I said, waving, as she backed out of the driveway.

The kids gathered around as I loosened the knot on the first bag. "Isn't it nice when people give us clothes?" I said.

My four-year-old peered into the bag. "There aren't any clothes in here," he announced. "It's nothing but a great big bag full of socks."

I gathered them into my arms—the children, not the socks—and hugged them. Isn't God good!

Dear Lord, thank You for faithfully meeting my needs. You are always there to help me when I reach out to You. I can feel Your steadfast love and care over me and my family. You are so good to us. Amen.

A Trusting Love

Le Ann Thieman

If I rise on the wings of the dawn,
if I settle on the far side of the sea,
even there your hand will guide me,
your right hand will hold me fast.

Psalm 139:9-10

As I placed the last few items into my suitcase, I could hear the radio in our bathroom, where my husband, Mark, listened as he shaved. "There have been reports of bombing within three miles of the Saigon city limits," the radio announcer repeated.

Mark came into the bedroom. We stared into each other's eyes, unable to look away, yet unable to speak. Then he quickly turned and left the room.

When I was approached about the possibility of escorting six babies from Vietnam to their adoptive homes in the United States, there had been no increase in the war for many months. Still, leaving Mark and our two chubby-cheeked little girls for two weeks would be difficult. When I asked Mark what he thought I should do, he said, "You gotta do what you gotta do, honey." But I knew the words, "Please don't go," were screaming inside him. I wondered how much restraint it had taken for him to silence his plea.

As I pondered my decision, I thought about the son Mark and I had applied to adopt through FCVN (Friends of the Children of Vietnam). Even though the adoption process meant a two-to-three-year wait, I couldn't help but believe it might mean something to our future son to know I had been to his homeland. Still, I called the U.S. State Department for advice. The man on the phone told me, "The war is not expected to escalate. Go!"

So after much thought and prayer, I agreed.

One week later, a tremendous Viet Cong offensive began. I doubt I'd have kept my promise to go if I hadn't had a powerful, faith-confirming experience in church on Easter Sunday, the day before I was scheduled to leave. I had been alone in prayer, kneeling as I rested my head on the pew in front of me.

"Please God, give me the courage I need to keep my commitment," I pleaded. Slowly, unexpectedly, a warm feeling enveloped me, and my tears began to subside. An inexplicable feeling of well-being filled me. I knew I'd be safe. God would take care of me.

Mark and I barely spoke during the thirty-minute drive to the airport at Cedar Rapids, Iowa. It was strange not to be able to talk about my leaving. We had always prided ourselves on our great ability to communicate. Mark was more than just my husband, he was also my confidant and best friend. There had never been anything I couldn't discuss with him—until now.

At the airport, we spent most of my pre-boarding time wrapped in each other's arms. When the final boarding call was announced, I lingered a little longer, hoping his love for me and trust in God were greater than his fears.

"I'll assume you're okay unless I hear from the Red Cross," Mark said, knowing phone communication from Vietnam would be next to impossible.

"I'll be fine," I assured him. Still, as I walked across the tarmac to board the plane, I couldn't bring myself to look back and see the pain I knew must be reflected on his face.

Once on board, I forced myself to look out the window and blow him a kiss. He returned it, trying to smile. I leaned back against the seat and allowed the tears to fall. Days later, when our plane finally circled Tan San Nhut airport and I saw camouflaged jets lining the runway, the questions and doubts echoed again until I was greeted by Cherie, FCVN's Saigon director. "Have you heard the news?" she exclaimed. "President Ford has okayed a giant, orphan airlift! Instead of rescuing six babies, you'll help rescue three hundred, if we're lucky!"

All the questions, all the doubts, were suddenly answered. I had a mission. God had clearly called me to be part of this rescue.

As Cherie drove through the overcrowded, chaotic streets, she explained how dozens of babies were being brought to the FCVN Center to get ready for the evacuation. Still, all my years as a pediatric nurse could not have prepared me for what I witnessed there. Every inch of floor was covered with mats, and every inch of mat was covered with babies! We spent the entire first day helping the Vietnamese workers diaper and feed scores of babbling, cooing, crying infants. Our night's sleep was shattered by the sounds of gunfire—harmless, the staff assured us. Still, as glad as I was to be on this mission, I was eager to complete it and get home to Mark and the girls.

So when I learned the next day that FCVN had been bumped from the first-place position to leave, I fought and argued to reclaim the first flight out—but to no avail. With disappointment still heavy in our hearts, we instead loaded babies destined for our Australian chapter. With twenty-two babies around me on the floor of a Volkswagen van, we headed for the airport. There we saw an enormous black cloud billowing at the end of the runway. A passerby told us that the first planeload of orphans, the one we had fought so hard to be on, had crashed on takeoff, killing half of the adults and children on board.

Stunned, we loaded the babies onto the Australian airliner, then returned to the FCVN Center. The office was awash with grief. I looked at my watch, still on Iowa time. The girls were having breakfast in their fuzzy pajamas. Mark was shaving and listening to the radio. I knew he would hear the news and be terrified, thinking that I had been on that flight. And there was no way for me to call and spare him this horror and heartache. I slumped onto a rattan sofa and sobbed uncontrollably. Several hours later, the phone rang.

When Cherie said, "Le Ann, it's for you," I almost laughed. Who would be calling me in Saigon? An Associated Press reporter was on the line. An Iowa reporter had contacted a chain of reporters across the Pacific to learn if I had been killed in the fatal crash.

"Sorry to tell you," the journalist said, "the Iowa newsman woke your husband to ask him if you were on the plane that crashed. But your husband hadn't heard the morning news, yet. We will get word to him that you are safe, I assure you." I began crying again, partly out of sorrow for the grief I was causing Mark and partly out of joy, knowing he would soon learn I was all right. Then, with renewed energy, faith, and confidence, I rejoined the workers preparing the babies for our flight—whenever that would be.

The next day at breakfast, Cherie sat beside me. "Le Ann, you and Mark will be adopting one of those babies in the next room. All your paperwork is here and in order. You can wait and be assigned a son from across the desk in the States, or you can go in there and choose a son yourself."

Speechless, I entered the next room and hopscotched through the sea of babies. Then, a little boy, wearing only a diaper, crawled across the floor and into my arms and heart. As I cuddled him, he nestled his head on my shoulder and seemed to hug me back. I carried him around the room, looking at and touching the other babies. I whispered a prayer for the decision I was about to make, knowing it would change many lives forever. "Oh, Mark, I wish you were here," I moaned. "How do I choose?" The little boy in my arms answered by patting my face.

"I know, son," I whispered into his ear as the realization hit me. I looked into his eyes and my heart melted. "I love you already, Mitchell."

Two days later, it was our turn to leave. The workers helped us load the babies onto a city bus, taking them to their freedom flight. We were nine volunteers caring for one hundred babies, placed three and four to a cardboard box. In spite of the stress, it was joyful work as we propped countless bottles and changed diarrhea diapers. Six hours later, we landed in the Philippines, where we were greeted by the American Red Cross.

"There is no phone access for you here," a gray-haired volunteer said, "but we will call your husband to let him know you're safe."

"He'll panic if he gets a call from the Red Cross!" I worried. Patting my hand, the nice lady promised me that he would be told in a reassuring manner. I hoped she was right. With a larger plane and more volunteers, we continued the next leg of our journey to Hawaii. There, every child was removed from the plane while it was refueled.

Finally, I saw an opportunity to call Mark, but the noise around the phone booth was so loud, I had to shout instructions to the operator. I mumbled to myself, "Mark doesn't even know we have a son. He has no idea I'm bringing him home."

I had rehearsed how I would tell him the wonderful news, but when I heard him answer, I could only blurt out, "Honey, this is Le Ann," and I started to bawl. I could hear him repeating my name as he, too, sobbed. I tried to compose myself so I could tell him about Mitchell, but I couldn't seem to catch my breath.

Then, still crying, he said, "Just tell me you're bringing me our son."

"Yes! Yes! Yes!" I cried, my heart bursting with excitement and love.

At the end of our long journey home, I carried Mitchell across the tarmac of the Cedar Rapids airport. Inside, we were mobbed by reporters flashing pictures. I could barely see Mark as he stepped forward and took Mitchell and me into his arms. In Saigon, I had feared that I would never feel his hug again. Now I didn't want to let go.

As Mitchell opened his arms and reached for his daddy, Mark hugged him to his chest, tears of joy filling his eyes. Then Mark drew me into the embrace as well. "Thank you," he whispered.

His love had trusted me every step of the way.

Dear Lord, please guide me through this journey of life. Thank you that no matter where my journey takes me, You will always be by my side. There is no place I can go to hide from Your love. You will never leave me nor forsake me. Amen.

My Father's Legacy

Dr. Jeanette Blanc

*We are God's workmanship, created in
Christ Jesus to do good works, which
God prepared in advance for us to do.*

Ephesians 2:10

The dean announced, "Jeanette Blanc, graduate with honors, Doctor of Philosophy."

My heart pounded as my black gown flowed in tempo to my graduation march. I had done it! I felt as if I were floating as I crossed the stage, my hand extended to grasp my hard-won diploma. As my faculty advisor draped the white and gold hood about my shoulders, it was as if the moment slowed in time. I was keenly aware of the proud faces of my husband, our two-year-old son, and my mother. I blinked. Was that a tear glistening in my father's eye?

Dad was a tough, fifty-four-year-old Vietnam vet who hid his emotions, but I could see his pride. His reaction confirmed that this was the most important accomplishment of my life. What I did not realize was that this would be one of the last memories I would ever have of my father's face.

Five days later, after all the hugs, celebrations, and congratulations, I rose to meet the dawn. Wrapped in my warm housecoat, I sat down at the table to share a cup of coffee with my father, before he and Mom left for their long drive home in separate directions. As we sat in the early quietness, my father leaned forward and placed his hand on mine.

"Jeanette, I was not a good father to you," he said. "I made so many mistakes. If I could do it all again, I would. But when I watched you walk across that stage, I saw you do something I never did. You embraced life. I'm so proud of you." He sighed and looked down at his wrinkled hand over mine. "It's too late for me. Even though I've been sober for three years and I've quit smoking, there's no time left to start over."

That's not true, I wanted to say. Yet the words wouldn't come. I could see the tired lines etched in his pale face beneath the fringes of his white hair. *When had he gotten so old?* I wondered.

My eyes followed him as he stood and walked across the room. When he turned back to look at me, his eyes seemed filled with regret. For a moment, we seemed to be frozen in time. Then, as if to prove his final words, his body slowly began to fall, crashing to the floor.

"Dad!" I screamed.

Desperately, I dialed 9-1-1. I gave him CPR for the fifteen minutes it took for the ambulance to arrive. The EMTs applied their defibrillator, jolting his body again and again, but it was no use.

"We're sorry. He's gone," they finally told me.

Grief overwhelmed me as I covered my face with my hands and wept. I was angry with myself for not being able to save Dad, to give him a second chance. But, most of all, my anger was directed at him. "Why did you wait so long to live?" I muttered as they covered his face with a sheet. But the time for words was over. Our time together was gone.

I grappled with my anger and despair for some time. But as the weeks melted into months, I chose to forgive both myself and my father, to let go of my bitterness. Now I cling to the lesson Dad taught me in his final moment. His legacy was to remind me how short life truly is. I now know I can't waste the time I have been given here on earth. I must set goals and be and do all I can to make a difference in the world.

Dad's lesson has continued to inspire me to love my family and reach out to speak to and teach others. My father may have lost his second chance, but his words were not too late to make a difference in my life. To the best of my ability, I will take advantage of the chance I've been given to embrace life fully.

Dear Lord, You inspire me to give out of the abundance You have given me. May my life make a difference to others, especially my family, friends, and coworkers. May I spend the time You have given me learning to know You in a deeper and more wonderful way. Help me to fulfill the purpose You have prepared for me. Amen.

Safe Harbors and Sailing Ships

Cynthia Fronk

From the fullness of his grace we have
all received one blessing after another.

John 1:16

I had been a registered nurse for about a year when I decided to move from my home in Milwaukee, Wisconsin, to take a job at a veteran's hospital in Prescott, Arizona. It was a lonely time—my first venture away from home.

I spent many evenings alone in my small apartment, worrying about how I would achieve my goals and wondering if the move had been the right decision for me? *Perhaps it would have been better if I had stayed in Milwaukee,* I often thought.

As I sat on my second-hand sofa, eating my dinner from a burger bag one evening, I began to think about home. I pictured myself in the kitchen with my mom, making delicious strawberry jam and grape jelly. Later, I could see myself sitting at the table with my mom and dad, and my brothers and sister, eating warm apple cobbler topped with dairy-fresh whipped cream. I missed the warmth of home and the love and security it represented.

One day, I was feeling particularly blue. Although I loved my job, my heart ached for my family. *Maybe I should move back home,* I reasoned.

That morning, while at work, I received a package in the mail from my father. He hardly ever shops, so I was surprised. *What would have inspired him to send me a gift?* I wondered. I tore away the brown wrapper, opened the package, and pulled out a poster silhouetting a large ship sailing into a blushing sunset. The words emblazoned across the gentle reflective waves touched me to the core. They said, "Sailing ships are safe in their harbor, but that's not what sailing ships were built for."

It was as if I could see my father's face smiling in approval. For the first time, my decision to leave home and set out on my own felt right. I knew my father, even though he was not a demonstrative, affectionate man, was trying to tell me that he missed me but supported my decision to go. He wanted me to be where I felt called to be, and he wanted me to do what I felt called to do. I knew I would sail farther still because my quest was championed by my father's love.

Mark Twain once said, "Twenty years from now you will be more disappointed by the things that you didn't do than by the things you did do. So throw off the bowlines. Sail away from the safe harbor. Catch the trade winds in your sails. Explore. Dream. Discover."

Dear Lord, please guide my ship through the storms of life and lead me to safe harbors. Thank You for the gales that make me stronger and the gentle breezes which bring me hope for tomorrow. Take me where You want me to be. Amen.

Encouragement

*Kind words are the music of the
world. They have power that seems
to be beyond natural causes, as if they
were some angel's song that had
lost its way and come on earth.*

Frederick William Faber

Healing at Columbine

Sandy Austin

*Just as the sufferings of Christ flow
over into our lives, so also through
Christ our comfort overflows.*

2 Corinthians 1:5

Screaming sirens. Hovering helicopters. Flashing lights. Yellow crime tape. No amount of training could have prepared me for what I was about to face.

Students streamed out of Columbine High School with hands on their heads like criminals. Mothers cradled shell-shocked daughters in their arms. Fathers frantically ran to embrace their sons. We stood transfixed in front of the television until our assistant principal gave us the following instruction, "All school district counselors need to report to Columbine immediately. Go!"

I hurried to my office, grabbed my coat and purse, and then ran to my car, turned on the radio, and headed toward Columbine. The sound of screeching tires pierced my consciousness as I swerved to miss a car that had cut me off. Many drivers were distracted by radio updates. The typical twenty-minute drive felt like an eternity. As I got to the main road leading to Columbine, I could feel the heaviness in the air. I prayed, *Lord, please give me the right words to say to each person. I don't want to say the wrong thing.*

Columbine was completely blocked off, and I was detoured to Leawood Elementary. The streets were filled with cars. An abandoned vehicle blocked a lane with its door open and signal lights still flashing. Streams of people heading toward Leawood darted between cars. Media vans jumped the curbs to park on the grass. Police from every jurisdiction swarmed over the area on the ground and in the air. I finally found a parking spot three blocks away. By then, the magnitude of the tragedy was beginning to set in. My heart racing, I quickly prayed, *Lord, please help me to calm down. Give me wisdom for each situation.*

I arrived at 1:30 P.M. and squeezed my way through the hordes of people. I flashed my ID and pushed my way through the main doors. Inside, chaos reigned. A familiar face directed me to the gym, where lines of parents, reunited and clinging to their kids, signed their names and hurried out of the building.

Confusion and frenzied activity now enveloped the gym—a stark contrast to the usual happy sound of elementary children at play. Students sobbed and hugged each other. Parents paced, eyes darting in search of their sons and daughters. Toddlers clung to their parents. Instructions broadcast from the front of the gym were drowned out by the shrill of ringing cell phones. Anxiety contorted faces, and fear crawled the walls.

Finally, buses arrived with the precious cargo from Columbine. As the students entered the gym, they were corralled onto the far end of the stage, where they could be seen. The joyful screams of relieved parents filled the room. But for other parents, the wait continued.

As I walked around the gym, I whispered a prayer, *God, lead me to the people You want to help through me.* A couple near the back of the gym caught my attention. The woman had soft, gentle eyes and an unpretentious demeanor. Her wind-blown, short brown hair hinted that she had been unexpectedly snatched away from her daily routine. She had the look of a mother who could relate to and understand teenagers. The man, dressed in business attire, must have rushed from his job to the scene. How did they hear about the shootings? For whom were they waiting—a son or daughter? What was running through their minds? *Lord, please reach out and comfort them,* I prayed.

Our eyes met briefly as I eased my way over to where the couple was standing. I introduced myself. "We are looking for our son Jake," she responded politely. "I am Karen Thompson, and this is my husband, Jim," she added. Sensing that they were too anxious to say more, I promised that I, too, would be listening for Jake's name and slipped away. The Thompsons personified the reserved hope mixed with fear that filled the room. I prayed as I walked to another area of the gym, *Lord, be with Jake wherever he is, and be with his parents also.*

During that terrible day, I talked with many of the parents and students as they waited for news. The names of students continued to ring out as the buses arrived. I listened for Jake's name, and when I failed to hear it, I would look across the gym to the Thompsons. Each time, they shook their heads. As the hours drug on, fewer buses arrived, and the atmosphere in the gym became more solemn. I checked in with the Thompsons as often as I could.

The gym was now swarming with people wanting to help. Tables overflowed with pizza, chicken, Mexican food, sandwiches, snacks, and drinks, but no one seemed to have much of an appetite. At about 6:30 P.M., a question rang out from the far side of the gym. "Are any more buses coming?" A deafening silence fell on the crowd. After a pause that seemed like forever, the answer came, "No."

My heart sank as I looked over at the Thompsons and saw their heads drop. They had several friends around them now, and I was glad to see that they had people to support them. Seventeen families sat in circles across the gym floor, waiting for word on their loved ones. Of the eight families with whom I worked most closely that day, six finally saw their children enter the gym—two did not.

The gravity of it all hit when police officials and the coroner announced that it would be hours before they would have final word on the remaining students. Parents were asked to provide detailed information about their sons and daughters, including dental records. Gasps rang out. The officials assured the parents that some children might still be hiding in the school, but at the same time acknowledged that there were definitely fatalities.

A while later, I watched as a woman was handed a blue cardboard box from which she pulled the plaster impressions of her son's teeth. The distressed woman grasped them in her hands for a few moments. Tears filled my eyes as I considered what she must be feeling, but I choked them back. I knew I had to stay focused if I intended to help those who needed me. Time to deal with my own grief would come soon enough.

Soon, a circle of praying people gathered around the Thompsons. I moved behind their circle but chose not to intrude, joining in their prayer from a distance. When they finished, Karen's friends urged her to go home to wait. I watched as she left with several friends at her side. Later, I learned that the Thompsons attended my sister's church. We were even more closely connected than I had realized. I believe that God specifically placed them on my heart so I could pray for them until their support network arrived.

Shortly after, Jim left for home, also surrounded by friends. At 9:30 P.M., I, too, left. Exhaustion hit me hard as I walked along the street. Yet the work had just begun. I would spend countless hours counseling students and parents in the days ahead.

Four days after the shooting, I saw a picture of Karen and Jim Thompson at their son's funeral on the front page of the morning paper. It brought back all the emotions of that day at Leawood. Once again I forced myself to keep them in check. I knew I would be counseling in the Columbine area throughout the summer and needed to keep myself strong for those who were depending on me. In the months ahead, however, I prayed every day for the Thompsons.

In the middle of the summer, I wrote Karen a letter to let her know she was in my thoughts and prayers. I knew that the most difficult times for those who have experienced a tragedy are typically three to four months after the event. By that time, the shock has worn off, and the grief is more intense than ever. Also, the constant support from friends and loved ones subsides as people are forced to return to their own lives.

A month or so later, I saw Karen at a women's conference in Denver. I had not seen her since that dreadful day in April, but I had thought of her every day. I was anxious to see how she was doing. To my surprise, I couldn't hold back my own tears any longer. But this time, Karen encouraged me. She said, "Sandy, your letter was a great encouragement. It came just when I needed it most. Knowing you were praying for me was such a comfort."

It comforted me to know that I had helped her, and I was glad to see how well she was doing. She had courageously faced her pain, and her example gave me strength to face my own pain. As I brushed away the tears that trickled down my cheeks, I knew that I, too, needed healing and the time had come. I now know with certainty that God will provide me the strength and solace I need to do whatever He calls me to do.

Dear Lord, You always have a plan to bring good, even from the most evil act. You are indeed the miracle maker. Use every situation in our lives for Your glory as we are careful to commit our ways to You. Amen.

A Davy Crockett Hat for David

Marjorie Evans

*And my God will meet all
your needs according to his
glorious riches in Christ Jesus.*

Philippians 4:19

"Mom-eee, I hurt! Mom-eee, hold me! Mom-e-e-e-!" Those were the cries I heard for days and nights. And my heart ached for my two little boys as I held their hot, feverish bodies on my lap and prayed the medicine would soon help them recover from the Asian flu.

Now they were recovering. Still congested, they breathed noisily as they napped in their beds across the room.

But then I got the flu. My body was drained of strength. I ached all over and tossed restlessly on my bed one gray, dreary December afternoon.

The flu was the least of my problems. There was no money to buy medicine, no money for food, and no money to buy gifts for the children for Christmas. Almost in despair, I breathed, *Lord, help me. I don't know what to do.*

When my husband left us, we moved across several states to be near my sister, who had agreed to help take care of my boys—David, five, and Charles, an energetic two and one-half year old. But the long move and days of looking for a job had depleted my resources.

The secretarial job I found barely provided enough money to support the boys and me. I had already missed several days of work and did not yet have sick leave. My sister's family was also striving to make ends meet and could not help us financially. As a Christian, I had faith in God and knew He had promised, "My God will meet all your needs according to his glorious riches in Christ Jesus" (Phil. 4:19).

But as my body became increasingly weaker, so did my faith. I struggled, *How, Lord? How can You supply when there's no money coming in?*

As I lay there, tears rolled down my feverish cheeks onto the crumpled pillow. I thought, *There's no way I can pay for medicine, but I have to have it.* Finally I called the drugstore. The druggist listened while I explained my situation.

"Don't you know that every cloud has a sliver lining?" he told me. "You're ill now and looking at the ugly black underneath side of the cloud. But one of these days, you'll be well again. Then you'll see the silver lining." The pharmacist told me I could charge the medicine and pay whenever I was able. "Have the doctor call in the prescription, and I'll send the medicine right over," he said.

After thanking the druggist, I called the doctor. Then I sank onto the faded green couch in our small, drab living room and prayed, *Thank You, Lord.*

Soon the medicine arrived, and it did help. A week later, although still shaky, I returned to work.

That day at lunch, my friends spoke eagerly about their Christmas plans and the gifts they had bought for their families. As they talked and laughed, I felt distressed about my inability to buy even one gift for my boys. The thought of the disappointment in their little faces on Christmas morning made tears well up in my eyes.

Then one of the women turned to me and asked, "What are you giving your children for Christmas, Marjorie?"

By now the tears were streaming down my face. Too choked up to answer, I fled to the women's lounge.

There I cried and cried until my good friend Mary came in. She questioned me until I poured out my troubles. Mary assured me everything would work out fine, but I couldn't see how.

The week before Christmas, I was more worried and distraught than ever. I wondered what we would do for food when the little we had was gone.

As I prepared our meager supper of tomato soup, crackers, peanut butter, and celery, I watched the children playing. Their little blonde heads bobbed up and down as they made their three-wheeled truck boom, buh-room, bump. Buh-room, bump, across the brown linoleum floor.

Suddenly David stopped, looked eagerly up at me, and said, "Please, Mommy, remember for Christmas I want a Davy Crockett hat with a tail, and I want a new truck, and I want some blue socks."

I looked down at the children and wondered how to explain to them that there would be no gifts. About that time, the doorbell rang, and I opened it to find Tom, an engineer from work, holding a big Christmas tree. Mary stood beside him, loaded down with packages.

What could I say? Overwhelmed, I just stood there. I felt like laughing and crying—and did both. Finally

Tom, his tender heart masked by his gruff manner, demanded, "Well, aren't you going to ask us to come in?"

The boys jumped up and down in excitement as Mary gave each one a candy cane and a gift. And she explained that the rest of the presents were for Christmas.

Eagerly, the children tore off the wrapping. David squealed with delight, "Mommy! Look! A real Davy Crockett hat with a tail." Putting on his hat, he began to sing about Davy Crockett as he proudly marched around the room.

Charles, his Crockett hat askew, chimed in, "Me Davy Kwockett, too, Mommy," and happily followed David.

Then Tom and Mary brought in a frozen turkey and all the trimmings for Christmas dinner plus bags of staple items. And they helped us decorate the tree.

When I tried to thank them, Tom interrupted, "A lot of us at the office got a real kick out of shopping for you and the boys. Believe it or not, giving to the three of you has given the rest of us a merrier Christmas."

Late that evening, as I sat on the old couch in our now festive and pine-scented living room, I talked to God. *Forgive me, dear Lord, for worrying about how our needs would be met. Not only did You provide what we*

*needed, You even provided a Davy Crockett hat for David
and one for Charles, too. Thank You.*

❧

*Dear Lord, You are my provider. Thank You
that I can trust You to provide for my needs with
Your glorious riches. You amaze me with Your
loving kindness. Your mercy endures forever. Amen.*

Go Tell Her I Love Her

Kathy Collard Miller

Encourage one another daily,
as long as it is called Today.

Hebrews 3:13

Sitting in the airport, waiting for my flight to leave, I couldn't seem to concentrate on my book. I kept glancing at the nearby snack counter wondering whether I should get something to eat. Suddenly, I sensed the Lord whisper in my heart, *Go tell the woman at the counter that I love her.*

Oh, Lord, You know I don't like to do things like that. People always think I'm weird, I protested.

I could sense the Lord waiting patiently. After trying to think of any good reason to refuse, I gave in. As I stood in line, I was surprised when no one else came up behind me to order. By the time it was my turn to order, no one was around except me and the fifty-ish woman behind the counter.

"May I help you?" she inquired.

"Yes, I would like a glass of iced tea," I responded. Hesitating, I suddenly felt the Lord's firm nudge. "But I also wanted to tell you that God loves you."

Her face registered shock.

Oh, no, I thought. *See what happens when You make me do this, Lord? Now I've offended her.*

Then in a second, her face softened and tears sprang into her eyes. She whispered through a choked voice, "You don't know how much I needed to hear that. My husband died three months ago, and I've been feeling like God doesn't care." She couldn't continue.

She fixed my iced tea, and when I went over to the attached counter to get some sugar, she followed me and poured out her heart about her grief. No one came up to the counter while we talked, and I was able to encourage her.

As we parted, she leaned over and hugged me.

I whispered a prayer as I walked away. *Okay, Lord. Just when I think You are just out to embarrass me, You take my reluctant obedience and use it for Your glory. Thank You!*

Dear Lord, help me be a willing servant. Show me how to reach out to others and give me the courage to act on Your direction. Thank You for the blessings that come to me when I follow Your instructions. Give me a spirit of boldness to serve You. Amen.

À Lapful of Lilacs

N a n c y   H o a g

My purpose is that they may be encouraged in heart and united in love, so that they may have the full riches of complete understanding, in order that they may know the mystery of God, namely, Christ.

Colossians 2:2

It seemed to me I needed a miracle.

Dressing for work, my mind was in a whirl, reviewing all the problems facing me. None of them were major—just an accumulation of "minor" irritations.

I was teaching at a small Christian high school where teachers not only taught but also served lunch, cleaned bathrooms, and directed "inspirational" chapel services daily.

My husband, whose work had taken him to Dallas, Nebraska, and even Nigeria, was off to India this time, and the very night he left, our car broke down at the shopping center—two miles from home. A friend towed it back to our driveway, where it would sit and wait for Scotty to come home.

Now, as I raced down the street in our second beat-up vehicle, the problems seemed to pass in review. There was the disabled car and finding time to take my daughter to her dance lesson, her voice lesson, and the orthodontist (who would see my child only during my working hours). It was also that time all teachers dread: semester's end and time for grades. It was time to decide if one should give a student the grade he's earned and risk spending an hour with his angry mother—or fudge a little in his favor, hoping he'll be encouraged and do better.

Furthermore, our dog—an accomplished escape artist—had tunneled under the iron gate and seemed to be daring everyone on the street to call the animal shelter again. Our cat had started spending his mornings in the neighbor's bird feeder, eating buttered toast while waiting for the main course to fly in. And my husband wouldn't be home for days.

It seemed it would take a miracle to juggle appointments, school grades, pets, and our temperamental truck until Scotty's return.

The school building was almost in sight when I rolled down the windows of the truck to let in the fresh air and caught the scent of lilacs. That wonderful fragrance reminded me of Spokane, Washington, where I'd grown up climbing trees and running through the pine woods with my best dog, Pal. I remembered my vow never to love anyone but Mike Nichols—even after sixth grade and even though my parents would soon be moving me to a place that felt like the other side of the world.

Lilacs. In Spokane they had grown wild in our yard. They'd flourished at Grandma's, too. Purple or white, they were—in my eyes—gorgeous. Lilacs were spring; lilacs were childhood play days. And, now, lilacs bloomed everywhere in Albuquerque—everywhere, that is, but in my yard.

Scotty and I had moved to New Mexico the year before, but we'd spent the planting season unpacking boxes, painting bathrooms, and "dog-proofing" the backyard. We were so busy that we hadn't planted a thing.

Gulping breaths of the lilac-scented morning, I began praying aloud. "Father," I said, "how I would love to have an armload of those lilacs! Enough of them to bury my face in! Enough to fill my lap!" I even confessed a longing to stop the truck, stretch across a stranger's fence, and pick lilacs until my heart was content. Instead, I resisted and drove on.

Pulling into my spot in the school parking lot, I grabbed my books, slid out of the driver's seat, whispered another quick prayer—this one about the taxing day ahead—and dashed through the double metal doors and right into a tall, gangly boy whose name was Kit. Shy and quiet, he wasn't one of the usual "greeters" who'd been following me to the classroom morning after morning with the hope of prying out of me what their grades would be.

"Good morning, Mrs. H.," he said.

"Good morning, Kit," I replied hastily as I hunched over the load of textbooks, standing first on one foot and then the other, all the while trying to pass by his lanky frame.

He smiled timidly. "I brought you something; it's in the kitchen."

Books crammed under my chin, the strap of my shoulder bag dangling at my elbow, I mumbled a "thank you," struggled down the poorly lit hall, dumped books onto my desk, and made my way to the kitchen for a large cup of black coffee. *Father, give me strength,* I moaned as I shoved the door open and stopped dead still as a strong fragrance engulfed me. It was not freshly brewed coffee and certainly not yesterday's unattended garbage. It was the scent of lilacs and, on the counter, I spotted an enormous bouquet—white and purple with a note that said, "Dear Mrs. H., Have a good day."

Dropping into a kitchen chair with the flowers in my lap and pressing my nose into the center of my surprise bouquet, I laughed; I cried; and I thanked my heavenly Father. I thanked Him for lilacs. I thanked Him, too, for the thoughtfulness of a student. I thanked Him for loving me, for answering "small" prayers, and for sending "little" miracles.

My courage bolstered and my faith revived, I walked back to my classroom with my arms full of lilacs, settled in my resolve to rest in my Father's love—despite our car troubles, our cranky dog, and our cat's determination to perch where our neighbor begged him not to. No matter how many appointments there were to juggle and how many grades had to be given out, I realized that God would give me the strength I needed to cope until my husband returned and every day after.

Dear Lord, we never know who is lonely of heart. Lead me to someone who could use a helping hand, a smile, a word of cheer. Help me to extend the gift of Your love to others. Amen.

Family

Home is where the heart is.

Pliny

A Generous Slice

Maureen Dreman and Sheila Seifert

I was hungry and you
gave me something to eat.

Matthew 25:35

While we cleared the feast from the table, I eyed the desserts on the counter. The strawberry and peach pies were tempting, but I was saving room for Aunt Edna's apple pie. Family reunions were not family reunions without a piece of Aunt Edna's homemade apple pie.

"Go ahead and relax in the living room," my mother said. "The kids and I will serve the pies in a little bit."

Uncle Ed told his cowboy tales in the corner by the stereo, while Selena and her new fiancé timidly propped themselves on the couch. Micki, my sister, walked past. "Bren's finally down," she announced. She looked exhausted. She had held screaming Bren during the entire meal.

"Do you get to rest now?" I asked.

"I get to eat now," Micki said. By the time I found a chair next to our second cousin Pat, Micki was back with a plate loaded with food.

"It's a little chilly in here," she said.

I pointed to the ceiling. "The vent's broken. I'll get an afghan."

"Thanks," Micki said as she sat down and took her first bite.

At the end of the hallway, I turned into Mom's darkened bedroom. Just as I reached the overstuffed chair, I realized the baby crib had been put in there and Bren was in it. The crib quivered. I froze. It quivered again. Relying on my knowledge of old combat-movie maneuvers, I hit the floor and rolled beneath the crib the instant Bren sat up. Surely she would go back to sleep soon. I crouched under the crib for several minutes . . . waiting.

The creak of the mattress told me that she was finally settling down. In slow motion, I crawled to the crib's side and slowly maneuvered out from under it. Only the cotton of my shirt betrayed me with a faint rustling sound. I went from a crawling position to a sitting position, hoping to eventually stand up and walk out.

Bren must have heard my traitorous clothing. She sat up again and then stood.

I had not seen some of my relatives since the previous year. *What was I doing wasting time playing a cat and mouse game with an eighteen-month-old child?* My sister's tired face came to mind, and I knew I had to get out of the room without causing Bren to scream for her mother.

Time ticked away as I crouched by the crib, the blood leaving my legs and cramps setting in. Then I heard the mattress creak. Bren was settling again. I maneuvered my way into a sprinting position. All was quiet. One, two, three. I silently counted before racing as fast as I could toward the hallway.

The moment I slipped through the partially closed door, I heard Bren move again but she did not cry. Within seconds, the mattress creaked, and she settled down.

"Was it worth it?" I asked myself.

In the living room, I caught Micki's eyes and smiled. She looked relaxed.

"I thought you went for a blanket," she said.

"Must have slipped my mind." I glanced through the kitchen door at two empty pie plates. It was still worth it, I decided. Turning, I watched Micki eat the last piece of Aunt Edna's apple pie.

Dear Lord, I pray that I will never be given my just desserts. Instead of giving me what I deserve, You give me love, mercy, and joy. Help me to show my thankfulness by being merciful to those around me. Amen.

For the Love of Daddy

Nancy Carter

*If one falls down, his friend can help
him up. But pity the man who falls
and has no one to help him up!*

Ecclesiastes 4:10

One morning, as I entered the shed in back of our house to get some nails, I saw my husband huddled in the darkness, drinking beer. I was horrified. It was only 9:00 A.M.! At that moment, I remembered something our son Bill had said to me. "Dad only makes sense early in the morning."

The next day when Bill dropped by, I asked him, "Do you think Dad's drinking is getting worse?" He didn't hesitate to answer. "Mom, yes. It's time to get help."

I soon realized that I'd known this for a long time. I just hadn't faced up to it. Really I hadn't known how. I still didn't. But one day, scanning the Yellow Pages, I saw a toll-free number for a recovery center for alcoholics, and I called. My call was transferred to a center near our home, and I gave the counselor a brief history of our situation. He urged me to make an appointment.

On that first visit, I gave more details about the twenty years Ray had been drinking. The counselor explained to me that alcoholism is a disease and urged me to initiate an intervention.

Almost one month later, I found myself sitting in the counselor's office waiting for Ray to arrive. I had asked him to come down to talk about a problem I was having. "I'm worried about our marriage," I explained. Though I had asked him many times over the years to go to counseling with me, he had refused. *Would he come now?* I wondered.

Bill brought Ray down and acted as if he had come along only to drop him off. When they walked into the room, my heart sank. *This is never going to work,* I fretted. I wanted to run. But there we all sat, fortified like a mighty army—one son, three daughters, two sons-in-law, two grandchildren, and a good friend. I knew other family members and friends were praying.

The room was electric with emotion. The counselor introduced himself. "Ray, the subject is alcohol. Everyone is here to talk to you because they care."

My hands were shaking. I knew everyone was nervous, but I worried, *Ray's white as a sheet. How is he feeling?*

The counselor asked Ray if he would be willing to sit down and listen. He nodded.

My friend spoke first. "Ray, I've been in your home countless times when you have been drunk," she said. "It's gone too far."

My sons-in-law voiced their concern.

Then Robin, our oldest daughter, told her father, "When I was a kid, you embarrassed me many times in front of my friends because you were drunk. I finally learned not to invite them to the house." She sighed. "Daddy, every time we come to visit, I tell you to take care of yourself, but what I have always wanted to say is 'please stop drinking.'"

"I remember all the times I went to horse shows with you," Donna, our youngest, said. "But by the time we got home, you'd be so drunk you couldn't put away the horses. I'd have to do it for you."

One by one, each person recounted painful experiences that had been caused by Ray's drinking.

Everyone was now crying—everyone but Ray. I couldn't imagine what he was feeling. He hadn't said one word or even expressed much emotion. Now it was time for me to speak the painful truth to my husband of thirty-one years.

In the course of our marriage, I had tried everything—talking, even lecturing. I had tried just being there for him. I had tried being a compliant doormat. I had even tried to leave him several times. But I always came home. I loved him.

In a choked voice I said, "Ray, remember the time I had to be rushed to the hospital for a blood transfusion? They told me you had been notified, but you didn't come—for hours. Later I learned that you were drunk. Do you know how that made me feel? It made me feel alone and unloved. I know I can't go through that again."

The last person to speak was Bill. "Dad . . ." he began, but he couldn't continue; his eyes filled with tears. After a moment, Bill found his voice. I took his hand and my husband's hand and squeezed them both tightly. "Dad, I remember all the times you'd come to my ball games to umpire. The other guys would laugh. You thought they were laughing *with* you, but they were laughing *at* you because you were drunk."

As the words of loved ones hung in the air, the counselor took over. "Ray, would you consider going into a recovery program?"

I was startled, even elated, when Ray agreed. He went into a twenty-one-day recovery program and never took another drink. His emphysema was advancing very fast at that time, but he became active in Alcoholics Anonymous and turned his life over to God.

Four years later at our Christmas gathering, we stood in a circle, as we always do, to have a Christmas toast. My son-in-law Rob turned to Ray and said, "A few years ago we attended your intervention, Ray, and I didn't know if it would last, but it has. I just wanted you to know I'm proud of you. You made that change, and we are all so thankful."

We all raised our glasses of grape juice and said, "Here, here." Ray lived only two more years, but during that time, he was able to help some of his buddies find sobriety. My final memories of Ray are happy ones. I am grateful that our family cared enough to intervene.

Dear Lord, give me courage to do the hard and needful thing. Keep my motivations pure and grounded in Your love. Thank You for being there when I stumble, and help me to reach out to others who have fallen. Amen.

Kidnapped

Verda J. Glick

He rescued me from my powerful enemy, from my foes, who were too strong for me.

Psalm 18:17

*O*ur lives as missionaries in El Salvador had become scary. Reports of killings were trickling in. We heard about a girl who had been shot in her car for not stopping at a checkpoint, and our son, Eli, had seen a pile of corpses beside the road. So when my husband didn't return after conducting a preaching service in the mountains, my heart was sick with concern.

I rushed to the door when I heard the tires of our oldest son's pickup crackle over our gravel driveway. I could see fear in his eyes as he climbed out of the cab. "What's the matter?" I called. "Is Papa all right?"

"Momma," Eli said as he strode toward me, "there's a problem." Putting his arm around me, he continued.

"Apparently robbers stopped Papa as he came down the mountain. They're asking for ransom. Momma, we hope he's all right." Eli and I walked through the front door together, and he pointed at the kitchen table. "Come, sit down. We need to talk."

My knees felt weak, and tightness spread across my chest. I was afraid to ask, but I had to know. I sat on the hard wooden chair and grasped Eli's hand as I pleaded, "What happened? Where is he? Did they . . . hurt him?"

Eli tightened his grip on my shoulder. "I don't know many details," he answered. "I only know that the kidnappers want $11,500."

I gasped. "So much money!"

"They demanded that I deliver the ransom alone tomorrow, before 2:00 in the afternoon," he said.

My thoughts raced ahead in fear, yet in my heart, I knew there was only one place to turn. "Let's pray," I urged, falling on my knees by the faded brown sofa. I wept as we asked God to protect Ernest.

As we knelt there, my favorite Bible verse flashed through my mind. "Lord," I prayed, "You are our refuge and strength, a very present help in trouble. Please spare Ernest's life. Help us know what to do."

I thanked God that Eli was with me. For the first time, our roles were reversed. Eli was strong; I was weak. He was caring for me; I was depending on him. I laid my head against his chest and wept as he wrapped his arms around me.

How could I let my twenty-three-year-old son go up that mountain to deliver the ransom? My love for my husband made me want to pay the ransom as quickly as possible. But my love for my son made me hesitate. I felt torn.

After an agonizing night of indecision, I accepted the fact that Eli would have to deliver the ransom. It was Ernest's only chance.

All too soon, the dreaded moment came. I clung to my firstborn son, finding comfort in the warmth and strength of his arms around me. *How could I let him go?* I felt a sob rising from the depths of my soul. *Oh God,* I prayed, *please protect Ernest and Eli. Bring them both safely home again. Please!*

I saw in Eli a maturity that had not been apparent before that day, but I also sensed he was afraid. What would he find on the mountain? We had both heard the stories of merciless kidnappers who murdered their victims.

I held on to him for a few moments longer, and then, remembering the deadline, released him. "Go, my son," I said brokenly, "and may God go with you." I kissed him on the cheek and handed him the package of ransom money. I watched as he got into the pickup and drove away. With a troubled heart, I turned to my heavenly Father, who had not spared His own Son but sent Him on a dangerous mission to pay my ransom. As I prayed, God filled me with strength and peace.

Hours later, I was elated when both my husband and son returned home safely. I took turns holding them in my arms and weeping for joy. God was faithful! Today, because of this page in our family's history, I have a deeper appreciation for God's love, for it sustained me in one of the most difficult situations I have ever faced. I will be forever grateful.

Dear Lord, Your own dear Son paid the ransom for my soul. How grateful I am for His gift. I give You my own life in return. Lead me daily as I strive to do those things that are pleasing in Your sight. Amen.

They're Mothering Me to Death

Eileen Herbert Jordan

*Even to your old age and gray hairs
I am he, I am he who will sustain you.*

Isaiah 46:4

"Take two teaspoons," she says, "every four hours." I open wide as she feeds me ruby-red liquid from a bottle in her hand. "It will control the cough, and it will loosen it, too. Just be sure you buy the right kind. Do you want to take this label with you so you'll know?"

No, I don't. I want something though. I am overwhelmed by a feeling of *déjà vu* gone mad.

The young woman standing there, pointing a spoon at me, issuing orders, defining my cough medicine, is my daughter. This is the child whose young chin I once held firmly until she swallowed her vitamins, the one whose whole medical history used to belong only to me.

"I took two aspirin when I woke up," I had told her earlier when she asked about my muffled voice. "It's a summer cold, and I will undoubtedly recover."

"Well," she said thoughtfully, "you could certainly do better than that." My daughter is a stay-at-home mother now and as a result, queen of the TV commercials, a princess of patent medicine. She opens her medicine cabinet door and ticks off a host of remedies for me to consider—Neo-Synephrine, Primatene, Dristan, Actifed, Contac, Benadryl, Ascriptin. There are more, but I don't hear them. I am too busy plotting my escape.

Just when you think you have survived the pitfalls of parenting, the very people you nurtured turn around and begin to try to parent you. Surviving their efforts to ensure your survival is no mean feat.

Our children belong to the exercise and pure-food generation. For them, food is not something wonderful but an amalgam of carbohydrates and magnesium, potassium and zinc, and fiber. Entire food categories are fraught with peril.

Take red meat for example. It is New Year's Eve, and I am sitting with my son and his wife in a restaurant in Old Town in Albuquerque, New Mexico. The room is so authentically Western I feel like Miss Kitty. When I move, I'm sure my skirts will swish. I open the menu, and the special of the night leaps out at me: *Prime Ribs of Beef au Jus.*

"The special is prime rib," I say after a minute.

They both nod. They look, well . . . not horrified, just pained.

"I know it's red meat," I say. But I have come a long way to visit them, and they are polite. I am prepared to brazen it out. After all, I was courted in some of the better steak houses in New York.

I order it. I eat it with guilt. I recall other times I have ignored their advice on health matters (bee sting therapy for my backache; a pillow filled with mugwort, white sage, hops, and bear root for insomnia). And here I am—failing food. The sidelong glances my son gives my plate as I eat my cholesterol-rich fare gives me the distinct impression he thinks my days are numbered.

When it comes to what I eat, I will stand my ground, though I have been known to eat my hamburger or Häagen-Dazs in private. When it comes to exercise, however, I tell them I just love the fitness program for older women they have found for me; otherwise, I know they will surely find another that is worse.

Or they will come up with another machine I should buy. As one who has never owned a car without power steering, why would I want to meddle with mechanical devices that make you push and pull and strain and hop and trot and rotate?

"The best thing for you would be a Stair Master," my son says.

I have spent years of my life schlepping up and down stairs. The laundry room was in the basement. The bedrooms were on the third floor.

There was a straw basket at the foot of the stairs where family members were supposed to pick up their clean clothes on the way up to their rooms. But the only one who ever carried that basket upstairs was I.

Today I live in an apartment where I glide horizontally from room to room. I may never climb a stair again.

"It's too bad I don't have room for a Stair Master," I say to him. "That's the trouble with living in an apartment."

Yes, I will cheat. I will feed their fiber cereal to the birds. I will pour their medicine down the drain. I will conceal my vices.

But, do you know what? I don't mind. While my contemporaries are reading the obituaries and cataloging their ailments in every conversation, my children are behaving as if, handled right, I could live forever— whether I want to or not.

Dear Lord, life is fraught with peril. We can't always trust our food, water, or even the air we breathe. But we can trust You. Give us the wisdom to know how to live a long and happy life. Amen.

Romance

To have and to hold from this day forward, for better for worse, for richer for poorer, in sickness and in health, to love and to cherish, till death us do part.

Book of Common Prayer

The Browning Romance

Christine E. Drews

Whither thou goest, I will go; and
where thou lodgest, I will lodge: thy people
shall be my people, and thy God my God.

Ruth 1:16 KJV

Since her fall from a horse at the age of fifteen,
Elizabeth Barrett continued to live at home, nursing an
injured back. Her father, Edward Moulton-Barrett was
solicitous concerning his daughter's medical needs, and
Elizabeth's sister often kept her company as she lay in
bed. The young woman's existence was tiresome and
dreary at best. When Elizabeth was twenty-two years
old, her mother died suddenly. The event only served to
increase Mr. Barrett's careful control over his daughter's
health and environment.

What little pleasure Elizabeth experienced in living came to her through books, particularly books of poetry. After a long and extensive study of the classics, she tried her hand at poetry. Her work was first published in 1838. It was titled *The Seraphim and Other Poems.* That same year, Elizabeth's health required her to relocate to Torquay in Cornwall. Her younger brother, Edward, her favorite, joined her there. She was utterly crushed later that year when Edward drowned. After returning to her father's house on Wimpole Street, she spent the next five years as a virtual recluse, seeing almost no one outside of her immediate family.

One of the few friends Elizabeth did occasionally see was a Mr. John Kenyon, who used his wealth to promote the arts he most enjoyed, including poetry. In 1844, she published another book of poetry, which created a stir in the literary world. Robert Browning, an up-and-coming young poet, wrote to profess his admiration for her work. However, Elizabeth steadfastly refused to meet him until her friend John Kenyon arranged an introduction in May of 1845.

Robert and Elizabeth established a rapport of the mind, spending the evening discussing literature and history. Their time together ended abruptly due to Mr. Barrett's rigid enforcement of his daughter's schedule. But a bond had been formed.

Elizabeth had roused the young poet's interest. They continued to meet under cover of her friendship with Kenyon, inasmuch as Mr. Barrett would never have allowed his invalid daughter to be courted properly. His intention was to keep her at home, under his watchful eye where she would always be safe.

As Elizabeth and Robert grew closer, she found it difficult to trust his words of love. He was six years younger, strong and handsome, with a promising career. When Robert proposed marriage, Elizabeth protested that her injury was too great an obstacle to allow them the happiness of married life. She asked that he remain content with their visits and correspondence, which had become the mainstay of her life.

Unwilling to agree to her reasoning, Robert continued to press. He was convinced that Elizabeth's injury was not as serious as she had always been told and that the opium she was being given as a medication kept her in her invalid state. He finally convinced her to decrease her medication, and after a few weeks of withdrawal, she began to feel stronger and healthier. Meanwhile, Edward had noticed the growing intimacy between his book-loving daughter and the young Mr. Browning. He soon forbade any more visits or correspondence, insisting that it was dangerous to Elizabeth's health.

Robert and Elizabeth continued to correspond via clandestine notes passed along by a family friend. It would be possible for them to marry, Robert insisted, but they had to act quickly, knowing that her father would never agree. Elizabeth considered her situation carefully. She was reluctant to show her father disrespect or embarrass herself and her family with a blatant breach of convention. On the other hand, she could not imagine her life without Robert. Together they devised a plan.

Elizabeth began to take carriage rides in the park with her sister to test her strength for the long journey ahead. In August 1846, she and Robert were married in secret. A week later, she left her childhood home with nothing more than her handbag and a few clothes. They headed for Italy, where they would spend their lives together.

The poetry of Robert Browning and Elizabeth Barrett Browning was enhanced by the richness of the art that surrounded them in Italy. She, out of a heart overflowing with happiness, penned the famous *Sonnets from the Portuguese.* These poems were such an intimate disclosure of her feelings for her husband that she felt she had to present them as translations of someone else's poetry originally written in Portuguese.

In light of Elizabeth's lifelong health problems, the Brownings never expected to have children. However, the warm climate and the assiduous attention of her loving husband worked a miracle in Elizabeth's life. She gave birth to a healthy son, Robert Wiedeman Barrett Browning, in 1849. Elizabeth was forty-three years of age and Robert was thirty-seven.

Their lives were lived out in the strength of their love for each other, which surpassed the confines of an overly protective father and the conventions of a rigid society. Their love for each other has since enriched the lives of countless other couples through the romance of their poetry. Love never fails.

How Do I Love Thee?

By Elizabeth Barrett Browning

How do I love thee? Let me count the ways.
I love thee to the depth and breadth and height
My soul can reach, when feeling out of sight
For the ends of Being and ideal Grace.
I love thee to the level of everyday's
Most quiet need, by sun and candle-light.
I love thee freely, as men strive for Right;
I love thee purely, as they turn from Praise.

I love thee with the passion put to use
In my old griefs, and with my childhood's faith.
I love thee with a love I seemed to lose
With my lost saints,—I love thee with the breath,
Smiles, tears, of all my life!—and, if God choose,
I shall but love thee better after death.

*Dear Lord, please weave my life into a tapestry
of love. May the colors and patterns create a work
of beauty, a gift to be shared with another. Show
me how to love those who aren't always so lovable.
For I want to love them, just as You love me. Amen.*

Until Death Do Us Part!

Barbara Loftus Boswell

He has taken me to the banquet
hall, and his banner over me is love.

Song of Solomon 2:4

Brian and I were involved in a serious relationship, but as a single mom, dating meant, more often than not, a family affair. There were many more grade-school basketball games, dance recitals, and family movie nights than romantic dinners for two!

So when Brian and I planned a real "date" one weekend, I was thrilled! We decided on a play called *Flanagan's Wake,* and Brian ordered the tickets. When Saturday arrived, we were off to the show, with kisses to my daughters and thank-yous to the baby-sitter.

The play we attended turned out to be an interactive show, where audience participation is enthusiastically encouraged. The men all wore name tags with their real names followed by "Patrick" and the women were all "Mary" someone. We, Brian Patrick and Mary Barbara that is, sat chatting happily as the actors entered the intimate venue from behind the audience.

"Boo-hoo," sobbed the grieving "widow" of the poor, deceased Flanagan as she walked toward us. Stopping next to my aisle seat, she took my arm and sniffled, "No one can comfort like me girlfriend, Mary Barbara. Coom and sit wit me, will ya?"

Wouldn't you know, I thought, *I'm the first one they pick on!* Playing along, I followed Fiona (the widow), the priest, and several other cast members to the small stage. I tried to look consoling at appropriate moments. After all, the entire audience was looking at me!

After sitting for a bit at Fiona's side as the play continued and the "wake" proceeded, I began to wish that I were back in the audience with Brian. Here we were on our big "date" and sitting thirty feet from each other!

My thoughts were interrupted by the widow asking me, "Mary Barbara, haf ya ever looved someone like I looved Flanagan?"

"No," I said, shaking my head.

"Well," she continued, "doo ya haf a special soomone to loove?"

Nervous beyond belief, I again shook my head and said, "No."

I could tell by her expression that I was not playing along the way she wanted me to, but I couldn't seem to say anything else!

"Tell me, Mary Barbara, did ya coome here to mourn Flanagan ahl by yerself?"

"Yes," I answered, the untruth slipping from my lips!

"Well, then," the "priest" jumped in, "who's that over there? I saw ya wit him earlier. Is that your broother, then? Bring her broother oop here!"

They had seen Brian and called him up to the stage! I couldn't help but think how nervous he would be in front of an audience. He was generally a shy person. An embarrassed look on his face, Brian walked forward and stood in front of the small stage on which I sat. I looked at him and smiled nervously as the priest spoke again. "Yer not her broother, are ya?"

"No," Brian quietly shook his head. I thought it was extremely amusing that we'd both been drawn into the play!

"Well, then," said the priest, "do ya have anything to say fer yerself?"

Brian grinned as he turned to me, and I suddenly knew exactly what was going to happen! I jumped to my feet as he began to go down on one knee, but he gently sat me back down as I laughed and cried all at once.

"Barb," he said as he held my hands in his and held my gaze with his smiling eyes, "I truly believe that God has written your name on my heart, and I love you with everything that's in me. So I'm here to ask you to marry me."

I was dumbfounded! I hadn't suspected for a single second!

"Of course I will," I whispered, tears in my eyes. "I love you, Brian!" We embraced and then walked to our seats in the audience as they clapped and congratulated us. I can barely remember the rest of the play. My head was in the clouds!

I never tire of sharing our engagement story. I love to tell people about how Brian asked me to marry him at an Irish wake!

*Dear Lord, You are the author of romance.
Please write and direct the romance of my life
to be loving and sweet. Help me to find romance
in our marriage and when I can't find it,
help me to be willing to create it. Amen.*

Tell Maggie I Love Her

As told to Robert Fulghum

Love covers over all wrongs.

Proverbs 10:12

A very old man—George—who had been placed in a nursing home by his family, was a sad case. Nobody ever came in to see him. One day he stopped talking and refused to leave his room. He was cooperative enough with the staff and functional enough to take care of himself. He continued to eat and bathe. But he became a mute recluse, sitting alone in his room in his rocking chair all day, staring out the window. The staff decided he had a right to live as he wished, so they let him be.

A woman resident—Maggie—had taken an interest in George, and when he disappeared, she went in to visit with him. He didn't seem to mind, but he didn't respond either. She had started working on a quilt and, over time, she moved her handiwork little by little into his room.

She spent her days sewing and telling her life story, while he sat staring out the window. She had been in Vaudeville. She had a million stories and was very happy to have someone to listen to her. Nobody knew what he thought. He sat and stared. She talked. Months went by.

When Maggie finished the quilt, it was put on display in the main lobby of the nursing home. People said it was one of the most beautiful quilts they had ever seen. She was especially proud since it was the only quilt she had ever made.

The same week the quilt was finished, George passed away.

In the drawer of his nightstand, the staff found an envelope marked, "To be opened when I die." The note inside said only, "Tell Maggie I love her." When they told her, she cried as if her heart would break. She had loved him, too. She had made the quilt just for him.

And that is why George was buried wrapped in Maggie's quilt.

Dear Lord, it is true that love covers all wrongs. Your love blankets me with peace. Your loving-kindness surrounds me. I am glad to be Your child. Thank You for Your care. Amen.

You Don't Bring Me Flowers

Nancy Kennedy

*Every good and perfect gift is from above,
coming down from the Father of
the heavenly lights, who does not
change like shifting shadows.*

James 1:17

I was beginning to think that maybe it wasn't me Barry loved at all.

It was my car.

Our anniversary was coming up, and I'd hinted for weeks about a pair of silver hoop earrings, leaving no doubt whatsoever about what I wanted for a gift. I even left the jewelry store's catalog open on my husband's desk, with the earrings I wanted circled in red. *No way* could he miss the message.

As the day approached, I oh-so-subtly brought our conversations around to the subject of silver hoop earrings:

"Speaking of the new tax laws, don't you think silver brings out the green in my eyes?" I said with a wink. "The washing machine man says we need a new hose. He also agreed silver earrings would go nicely with my silver watch." And then, I cinched the deal with, "The gold market's down, but *silver.* . . ."

Finally our anniversary arrived and Barry's gift along with it: a set of tires for my car.

"Nothing but the best for my girl," he said, his chest puffed with male pride.

No silver hoop earrings. No lingerie. No boxes of Godiva chocolates. No flowers. No romantic expression of eternal devotion and undying commitment.

He had bought me tires—steel-belted, radial whitewalls to be exact. I remember staring at his silly grin and wondering if maybe his mother had dropped him on his head one too many times.

"Well?" he asked, still grinning. "Do you like them?"

I must have mumbled something like, "Oh, yes, yes, YES I do—I DO love them," because he kept grinning for the next hour or so while he washed and polished my car.

I, on the other hand, was *not* grinning. I sat on the porch and sniffled in self-pity. *Where's this man's sense of romance? Is he intentionally sadistic or just an insensitive clod?* We had a definite lack of understanding going on. It wasn't the first time, either. When it comes to buying each other gifts, Barry and I have a history of missing the mark.

Take the first birthday present I ever bought him. I'm ashamed to say it, but (now remember, back then these were all the rage) I bought Barry a powder blue, polyester leisure suit with patch pockets and a matching polyester belt. It wasn't easy hiding it from him, either. I put it on layaway at the men's store in town and paid ten dollars at a time for weeks.

I was overwhelmed with excitement as his birthday approached. I knew he'd open the box, take one look at it, and be eternally grateful to me for choosing such an incredible outfit for him (especially since his taste ran toward gray sweatpants and T-shirts).

On the morning of the big day (I think it was his twenty-third birthday), he sat at the kitchen table reading the newspaper. He came across an ad for the very same suit that I had all wrapped up and waiting for him in the hall closet. I'll never forget what happened next. He scoffed and said, "Can you believe this? Who would ever wear one of those things?"

I gulped, twittered, then hot-footed it back to the men's store, where I mumbled to the saleslady some lame excuse about my husband developing a sudden allergy to polyester and got my money back. I ended up getting him a set of drill bits and a box of Milk Duds, both of which he loved.

Another time—I think it was Mother's Day—(it was so traumatic I've blocked out the details) Barry bought me a vacuum cleaner. Not just any vacuum cleaner, but a huge monstrosity, a "home maintenance center." It had an attachment for everything, including one for painting the house and another for shampooing the dog. The girls oohed and aahed. Laura pretended it was a spaceship and rode around on it all afternoon. I, on the other hand, found it awkward, heavy, and a real pain to haul around the house. But Barry thought it was the *perfect* gift. He polished it, made me a pegboard on which to hang all the attachments, even offered to name it for me. I just shook my head and forced a smile.

To be fair, I have to admit my old vacuum cleaner had broken and I was constantly borrowing the neighbor's (not to mention whining about needing a new one), but that's not the point. The point is, he bought me a vacuum cleaner for Mother's Day!

I thanked him, then growled the rest of the day. It was the same growl I gave as I sat on the porch watching him wash and wax my car. If he really loved me (sniff, sniff), he would have known what I really wanted. Ever so often, Barry—unaware that our whole marriage was about to fall apart—would smile and wave as if nothing were wrong. It was all terribly pathetic and tragic.

But then, as I watched him scrubbing away at my car, my mind drifted back to our first date and how he searched all over northern Maine for size-seven ice skates because he'd promised to take me skating.

Then I remembered the time he bathed, dressed, and carried me to the doctor when I hurt my back and how he slept on the floor next to me, so I could be comfortable alone in the bed and he could still be near me.

Other images of Barry came to mind: letting me drink the last Diet Pepsi, shivering in the cold after giving me his jacket to wear, pretending to like—and even wearing—the shirt I made him the first year we were married. It's true, he's never given me jewelry, red roses, or a box of chocolates for any holiday, but does that necessarily mean the guy doesn't love me? Maybe it just means that we don't speak the same dialect when it comes to love.

As Barry rubbed wax on my car, I considered the possibility that his choice of gifts was truly an expression of love—namely, his concern for my safety. To be honest, I had noticed my tires were getting bald, but I'd probably never think to buy tires on my own. And even though I hadn't yet needed the snakebite kit or the road flares he'd given me, the jumper cables had come in handy a time or two. I used the vacuum cleaner every day.

Maybe the guy's okay after all, I concluded. Besides, as pretty as they are, flowers die. And as good as it tastes, chocolate goes directly to my hips.

My anger subsiding, I picked up a rag and helped polish the back bumper. The moment might not have made a Hallmark commercial, but with the sun's rays streaming through the clouds while I worked alongside my husband, it seemed incredibly romantic to me.

Our anniversary has passed now, but my birthday's approaching. What I'm hoping (and hinting) for this time is something pink and silky from Victoria's Secret. What I'll probably get is a tire gauge or a socket set.

That's okay. So what if I have a husband with an unconventional sense of what's romantic! I know he loves me. Just like he knows—polyester leisure suits notwithstanding—that I love him, too.

Of course, there's still the matter of my upcoming birthday. Just in case Barry decides to do something wild and crazy and surprise me with a more traditional gift, I think I'll leave the Victoria's Secret catalog on his desk.

Then again, maybe I'll just go buy something pink and silky and surprise him.

Dear Lord, help me not to keep my husband in hot water. Instead, teach me to forgive so I do not become hard-boiled. Help me to have a warm heart instead of a hot head so I will appreciate this man You have given me. Amen.

Sweethearts and Heroes

Rachel Hodges

These three remain: faith, hope and love.
But the greatest of these is love.

1 Corinthians 13:13

I sat in the backseat of my parents' car, the vial containing my mother's heart medicine resting safely in my pocket. We were, once more, on the way to the hospital. Despite her earlier refusal to enter the hospital again, the pain and discomfort had finally worn down my mother's strong spirit. I had had to bend low to hear the barely audible whisper, "I'll go to the hospital."

My heart ached for this dear woman, who had already suffered so much. Helpless in the face of her illness, I had sat with her for three days as she fought to stay at home. My two sisters were also there, and once Mom agreed to go, our thoughts centered on how to get her to the hospital as quickly and safely as possible. We would have called an ambulance, but Mom, even in her weakened condition, had already decided otherwise. "I want your daddy to take me," she said.

Concern for my mother's health was mixed with concern about Dad's driving. He had always been a good driver, but he was eighty years old, and the trip to the hospital involved traveling on the interstate highway. I wondered how well he would be able to drive in this tense and emotional situation.

Mother wanted him to drive. He wanted to drive. I loved both of them—what could I say?

Carefully, we placed Mom in the front passenger seat. Dad got in on the driver's side, and in silence, I got into the back. My two sisters would follow us in another car.

Dad checked the seat belts and started the car. I sensed his nervousness and saw it betrayed in the slight trembling of his hands on the wheel. All my qualms about Dad's driving resurfaced. *This was too much stress for him! Why hadn't I insisted on calling the ambulance?* Then the car began to move forward as I clutched the bottle of pills in my pocket.

I mentally rehearsed what I should do if Mother suffered a heart attack on the way. Silently, I asked God to be with her and comfort her, to help Dad drive safely, and to keep us all in His care. *Just let us get to the hospital, Lord,* I prayed deep in my soul.

As I rode with my parents, my mind, like a separate entity, took in the scene before me. My mother, so frail and thin at ninety-five pounds, her head covered with beautiful silver curls, sat slightly slumped forward in her seat. I saw the deep hollow in the back of her neck and the way her coat seemed to almost swallow her into its depths. I stifled a cry that only I could hear as it rose up inside me. *Oh, God why?*

I tried to subdue the pain in my heart and shifted my gaze to my father. A favorite brown hat rested on his thinning hair. Underneath the familiar brown jacket, he wore a green shirt I had given him years before. Despite its faded condition, Dad wore it often. Lines of age creased his face, and his jaw was not quite so firm as that of the young man he had once been. I saw his nervous swallow and understood what a tremendous sense of responsibility he felt for the welfare of his wife.

I sat there overwhelmed by a sense of being powerless to help either one of them. Then I saw two elderly hands reach across the space that divided the front seat. Mother's thin hand, with the veins so prominent and the fingers so slender that her wedding band needed tape to keep it from falling off, reached toward her husband's. My father's hand, weathered and aged by a life of hard work, gently closed around his wife's.

"Don't worry, honey," Dad said. "I'll get you to the hospital safely. I'll take care of you."

"I know you will," came Mother's soft reply as she gave him her gentle smile.

With the rare flash of insight God occasionally allows us to experience, my aching heart understood. The same love that had outlasted the years now colored their vision of each other. When Dad looked at his wife of almost sixty years, his eyes still saw the beautiful young woman he had courted and married. To Mother's eyes, Dad was still the bold and handsome young man with whom she had fallen in love so long ago. She was still his sweetheart, and he was still her hero. This was the gift of their enduring love.

Determined not to interrupt the special moment between them, I turned my face to the window so they couldn't see the hot tears that silently tracked down my face. That was my gift to them.

We finished the trip in silence.

My mother survived to return home one last time. A month later, she made her final trip to the hospital. Ironically, after all the years of worry about her heart problems, complications following surgery for a shattered hip finally claimed her life.

Even as I try to face the pain of my loss, I know I will never forget the sight of those two dear hands clasped together in love and caring.

Dear Lord, thank You for giving us dear relationships with our loved ones. Today, may we build sweet memories to cherish with one another in days to come. May our hands always be clasped in love. Amen.

Forgiveness

When you forgive, you free your soul.

Erica Wise

What Love Means

Rudy Galdonik

Forgive, and you will be forgiven.
Luke 6:37

My husband is a butcher. No, he doesn't earn his living by carefully slicing and dicing meat carcasses into delicious morsels. He prefers to work in the backyard with a trimmer, clipper, pruning shears, and the ever-effective chainsaw!

I was a widow with two small children when God chose to give me a wonderful gift—the man I now call my husband. I was delighted to have Mike around, especially when it came time to give the trees in the backyard their annual trimming.

We selected a perfect crisp, cool day for this project. For the first part of the morning, I left Mike to his work while I took care of my weekly errands. As soon as I returned, I headed over to where he was busy clipping an overgrown bush.

"Look over there and tell me what you think," Mike called out as he saw me approaching. Together we headed toward the back deck, where he pointed toward two large evergreen trees. I was so startled by what I saw that I let out a scream. My husband had reduced the tall, elegant evergreens to mere stumps with only an assortment of sticks poking out in every direction.

"What happened?" I blurted out in shock. Anger began to well up inside me as I stared with my mouth hanging open. It had taken years for those trees to grow tall and strong, providing the perfect visual screen between our deck and our neighbor's deck. Now they looked like lollipops!

Without speaking, I left my bewildered husband on the deck and pushed my way into the garage. My young son had heard my scream and scampered along behind me. "But, Mom," he asked, "is it really that bad?"

"Yes, it is," was all I could muster as a response.

I headed into the kitchen and proceeded to make lunch, banging cabinet doors and anything else I could get my hands on. But as I worked, my son's words continued to ring in my ears.

We ate lunch without a word being spoken. As Mike distracted himself by flipping through a flier, I toyed with my food, remembering a day not too long ago when I had walked down the aisle to meet this man. I remembered how he had beamed with love and joy as I approached. I also remembered my own feelings of excited anticipation as I considered what our lives together would bring. And now I was prepared to ruin this beautiful day and perhaps a whole weekend with my anger.

Would my anger return every time I stepped out into my backyard? Where would it all stop? Had God used my son's words to point to my error? Was it really all that important? I wondered.

I knew I needed to say something, but could I do it in a way that was pleasing to God? I prayed and took a deep breath. Then I looked over at my husband and asked, "Whatever possessed you to. . . ." Mike caught me in mid-sentence and slowly said, "I'm so sorry." The anguish he felt was clear in his eyes. "I just wanted to please you."

It turned out he had decided to crawl under the evergreens and give them a good cleaning out—not realizing that the brown, dead-looking branches underneath were actually the branches which were green and full on the outer edge of the limbs. "Once I started to snip, it was tough to know where to stop," he confessed.

I clearly knew he had intended no harm. He had volunteered to give up his Saturday to do landscaping, not because he enjoyed it but because he wanted to please me. I started to laugh as I slowly shook my head. God calls us to love for "better or worse," and when we are faced with a challenge, He provides us the ability to make it right. If that includes living with two sick-looking trees in the backyard, I guess it's a small price to pay.

Dear Lord, we all make mistakes. Please forgive me for my mistakes, help me forgive others for theirs, and help them to forgive me as well. Teach me how to make wise choices and decisions so that I may live my life in a way that is pleasing to You. Amen.

Coming Clean

Nancy Hoag

*If he sins against you seven times in
a day, and seven times comes back to
you and says, "I repent," forgive him.*

Luke 17:4

My husband had begun traveling three weeks out of
four. We'd prayed for a job change, a move where the
pace would be slower and our time would belong to us.
But the answer had been "no." To add to my
frustration, the weather hadn't been friendly. Fifteen
degrees below the springtime norm, crabgrass had taken
over—along with dandelions, grubs, and moles.

Now, after what seemed like too much rain and too
much time alone, I wanted to be comforted. I'd been
living on popcorn and fast food and looking forward to
cooking for and talking to someone other than myself.
My husband, on the other hand, had been in meetings,

arbitrating, trying to make first one and then another flight. He wanted to be left alone.

I don't remember which last straw did it, but I do remember bounding down our cellar stairs, jaws clenched, and seizing a comforter—one I'd stuffed into a bag months before because it didn't fit my washing machine. It was now my excuse to run away from home. If Scotty wouldn't listen, I'd retreat to reading and candy bars while the commercial washer did what had to be done.

The comforter spinning, I seated myself on a plastic chair. Snapping pages forward then back, I tried to concentrate on the magazine, but I couldn't quit thinking about my inconsiderate spouse. The man hadn't listened to one word I'd said. Yes, I understood these separations made life difficult for him, too. But that didn't negate the fact that he was insensitive.

"Men! They're all alike!" I'd murmured when I spotted a woman who'd once waited on me at a discount store. Looking weary and old before her time, she was loading not one washer but eight. Odd for someone who always looked as if she had "nothing to wear."

While I watched, she trudged to the coin machine, bought soap, returned to reserve a string of washers, jammed coins into cartridges, dumped detergent, slammed lids, slapped plastic baskets down on the concrete floor, and lit a cigarette.

She worked all day, everyday? Now she would spend her free time doing eight loads of laundry? At our house, we seldom had more than two. Much of what my husband wore, he took to the cleaners so I wouldn't have to deal with it.

I pictured Scotty with his arms full of jackets and slacks—grinning, asking if I wanted to ride along, proposing breakfast out or coffee on the way home.

But, this morning, he'd made me so mad.

I'd no sooner set my face like flint, when the other woman's husband suddenly appeared—shoulders slouched, billed cap on tilt, denims hanging from nearly invisible hips, a brown cigarette in one corner of his mouth, and wearing a frown. He hadn't said one word to his wife when two teen-aged girls bounded through double doors to join the pair.

Oh, good, I thought, *they're all going to help.* But they weren't. The girls wanted money for a pop machine, the man wanted multiple kisses planted on his skinny mouth. Giggling, the daughters departed while the man leaned against a washer to coach his wife. *Maybe he's just waiting until he's finished his smoke, then he'll give her a hand. Scotty would,* I breathed.

I continued to watch this husband and wife who weren't yet functioning as a team. The man was lighting another cigarette, while his wife literally ran from washers to dryers and back. *Help her!* I wanted to shout, *Scotty would!*

"You gonna be done pretty soon?" the sullen man asked, as if he had plans and his wife was holding him back.

For the next half hour, the woman worked and the man watched and tapped his lips with his forefinger when he wanted another smooch. Their daughters exited and returned at predictable intervals to announce they needed more cash and wished their mother would, "Hurry up."

I don't believe this! If I had all that wash, Scotty would never expect me to manage alone. The nights he was home, didn't he dry the dishes for me? And what about mornings? While I cooked breakfast and packed his lunch, didn't he make the bed? When he needed a shirt, didn't he usually iron it himself? Had he once complained?

The other husband's abrasive voice interrupted my new self-awareness. "Maybe I'll go see what the kids are up to," he said.

"Go see what the kids are up to?" I exhaled. "Help your wife!" I stood straight up out of my chair. "Scotty would," I said aloud, stepping toward my dryer. Just then, Scotty walked through the door and seemed to fill the room.

He was still wearing the faded shoes he'd donned to dig in his garden because "gardens can't wait!" He wore the goofy shirt he'd "captured" from my giveaway bag because he planned to root poison ivy out of my flower bed. "It won't disappear by itself," he'd said.

"Scotty! Why are you here?" I blurted, thinking how even when he was agitated, his blue eyes gave away his tenderness.

"Babe, I haven't been very good to you." He cleared his throat and stuffed his hands into his denim pockets, looking like the cowboy he'd been when we'd met. I wanted to fling my arms around his neck. I felt like the heroine in a Western romance.

"You are much more important than any garden," he said, squeezing my hand. "Besides, it gets lonely at home when you aren't there."

I wouldn't cry and I wouldn't kiss my husband in a Laundromat, but I was tempted.

"Is your comforter done?" Scotty asked.

I'd forgotten I owned a comforter.

"I just have to fold it and then. . . ."

But Scotty wasn't listening. He was walking away. "Come on, babe," he said, smiling over his shoulder. "I'll give you a hand." At the dryer door, he began unwinding the tulips and leaves. "I'm taking you to lunch," he said, reaching across the fabric to squeeze my hand.

I glanced at the woman whose wash was nearly dry. She'd be folding forever. I glowered at her spouse who was grumbling something about "going for ice cream with the girls." I touched Scotty's face where his laugh lines begin, no longer caring what strangers thought. Kissing his cheek, I told him I was sorry, I loved him, and I was grateful for the marriage we shared.

Our folding finished, I admitted I'd been having more than a little trouble with the frequent separations.

"Me, too, babe," Scotty said, his palm warm and comforting at the back of my neck.

I turned sideways to catch one last glimpse of the man squinting at his watch and tapping his boot as he waited for his wife.

I tucked my fingers into Scotty's as we headed for the door.

"I'm glad you're my husband," I whispered, "even if you do travel," I said as I felt Scotty squeeze my hand.

Dear Lord, only You can fill that God-shaped hole in my life. Forgive me when I try to fill it with my expectations of my friends and family. And help me to be thankful for what You have given me. Amen.

Faith Walk

Linda Evans Shepherd

Repent, then, and turn to God, so that
your sins may be wiped out, that times
of refreshing may come from the Lord.

Acts 3:19

Recently, I heard a speaker talk about the cruelty our country's white forefathers spawned toward their black brothers and sisters. As she talked, I felt my cheeks burn. My great-great-greats were slave owners from the South. *But these people seemed so far removed from me. Was I still connected to their long-ago injustices?* I wondered.

I stung with shame as I listened to the speaker list their crimes. I felt sorry to somehow be connected with these stories of oppression. When the congregation bowed their heads in prayer, I prayed, *But, Lord, what can I do now? I'm not responsible for my forefather's actions, am I?*

Feeling somehow justified, I concluded my prayer and raised my head. That's when my heavenly Father guided my attention to a black woman, dressed in a pale green suit, sitting near me.

Apologize to her, He directed.

But this woman and my forefathers are strangers to me, I argued. *Am I responsible for what took place more than a century ago?*

Apologize anyway, God seemed to speak to my heart.

After the service, I stalked my unsuspecting sister. I trembled with relief when she didn't notice me. After all, what was I supposed to say to her? *My forefathers owned slaves and I'm sorry!* I followed her to the book table and watched her browse. I noticed her grimace as she searched her purse. Her expression told me she had forgotten her checkbook. As she turned to leave, I grabbed my opportunity and purchased the book she wanted. Quickly, I followed her to the other side of the auditorium. Feeling somewhat foolish, I thrust the book at her.

"Pardon me, but I want to give this to you," I said.

Her brown eyes widened, and she looked into my pale face.

"The Lord spoke to me and told me to apologize to you," I continued, knowing she'd either reject me or think I was crazy. Her eyes held steady.

"Apologize for what?"

Blushing with shame, I explained, "You see, my forefathers owned slaves. I'm really sorry. I feel the Lord wanted you to know how I felt. Will you forgive me?"

Her eyes filled with tears, and she surrounded me with her arms. "I do forgive you," she cried.

After our tearful hug, she looked at me and smiled, "I'm so glad I came to church today. I almost stayed home, but the Lord told me that if I came, He would do something special for me, and He has. He sent you."

I smiled, too, relieved by her acceptance and excited to know that I had heard God's voice. But the most amazing thing was, in my obedience to God's nudges, I received a gift, too. I made a new friend.

Dear Lord, give me courage to right wrongs whenever I can. Show me how to go the extra mile to do what's right. Fill me with Your courage, and give me a spirit of boldness so that I will not be ashamed to reach out in Your love. Amen.

Thimble of Love

Carolyn Standerfer

*Be kind and compassionate to
one another, forgiving each other,
just as in Christ God forgave you.*

Ephesians 4:32

My dad's long-overdue admission that he had molested me throughout my childhood made no difference at all. It was just too painful for my mom to face.

Why can't she give me the love and support I need and deserve? my heart cried out. I felt betrayed. My mom felt blamed. All attempts to make peace failed. Soon pain and anger ran like a raging river, eroding the banks and widening the gap between us.

After two long, cold years of silence, a day came when we were to be at a gathering together. The hour drew nearer. Like frightened deer with nowhere left to run, we faced the great chasm of silence that gaped between us.

"Grandmother!" my eight-year-old daughter, Sarah, squealed as she jumped out of the car. Her ivory arms and golden hair swept about the Grandma she loved and missed so terribly. "I have a present for you," she announced with delight. She opened her little hand slowly before her grandma's wondering eyes. "Mommy bought it," she whispered.

My silver-haired mother caressed the tiny china thimble. She gently touched the delicate flowers and "Grandmother" that were painted on it in beautiful pastels.

"Be careful, Grandmother," Sarah warned, "it's very fragile."

"That it is," she replied. "It's lovely! Thank you." She bent to kiss her granddaughter's silken head. Then turning toward me, she reached out a trembling hand. Without a word, I moved into her embrace. Unbidden tears slipped quietly down my cheeks.

"Thank you, too," she breathed. "I will treasure it."

A small gift. A fragile beginning. But our God has been known to do great things with even less. That thimble was full of forgiveness, acceptance, and mercy. A thimble full of love. I wonder—*if a mustard seed of faith can move a mountain, can a thimble full of love fill a chasm?*

Dear Lord, thank You that a thimble of love can fill a chasm. Please teach me how to forgive and re-forgive as many times as necessary. Thank You that Your forgiveness covers me. Amen.

Children

*Like a rose, a child will blossom
when cultivated with love.*

Anonymous

Listen with Your Eyes, Mommy

Susan Titus Osborn

*Train a child in the way he should go, and
when he is old he will not turn from it.*

Proverbs 22:6

Running into the kitchen, my son chattered on as he held the birdfeeder he was building. "Look, Mommy. See the little perches? I sanded them smooth so the birds won't hurt their feet," Mike said excitedly.

Up to my elbows in dough, kneading it as he spoke, I said, "Uh-huh." Mentally I reviewed the dinner menu, checking off each item to make sure everything would be ready at the same time.

Mike continued his chatter.

"I wonder what kind of birds will come and eat? It's almost finished, Mommy. Let's go buy some birdseed tomorrow. Doesn't the birdhouse look great?"

Every few minutes I said, "Uh-huh," to show Mike I was listening, but my thoughts were far away.

"What color should I paint it, Mommy?" Mike asked. When he received no reply, he suggested, "Red, or maybe blue, or maybe white with blue trim like our house? What do you think, Mommy?"

Glancing at the clock, I realized that my dinner guests would arrive in half an hour. The bread wouldn't be ready. I wasn't dressed and hadn't even thought about what I would wear. As my mind whirled with these thoughts, my son went on.

"Where should we hang it, Mommy? On the tree? On the patio? Where, Mommy? Huh? Mommy, are you listening?"

Suddenly Mike's pleading tone caught my attention. I looked down into his huge blue eyes brimming with tears.

"Mommy, I want you to listen to me," he begged.

"I am, dear," I replied as I folded the dough into a pan.

"No, Mommy. You're not listening. You're not listening with your eyes," Mike said softly.

Suddenly I realized what my young son meant, and I knew he was right. I placed the dough in the oven and washed my hands. Then I bent down and hugged Mike.

"Now I'm listening with my ears and my eyes." I promised. "Why don't you paint the birdhouse white with blue trim so it will match our house. There's some leftover paint in the shed. I'll show you where it is before I get dressed."

The dinner guests could wait.

Dear Lord, teach me to pay attention to those small faces You have put into my life. Teach me to sit and talk to them, to run and play with them, to giggle and laugh with them. But most of all, help me teach them to know what is really important in life. Amen.

Breakdown!

Betsy Dill

*May the LORD answer you when you
are in distress; may the name of the
God of Jacob protect you.*

Psalm 20:1

Late one raw February night, the fuel pump exploded under the car hood with a gigantic thump. The steering wheel developed a will of its own and fought back. I experienced instant terror, as I wrestled the car to the side of the road and watched billowing clouds of acrid smoke plume in front of the windshield.

"OUT!" I screamed to my ten-year-old son, and we ran back ten feet before I realized the key was still in the ignition and my pocketbook was on the seat. I dashed back to grab my keys and purse before retreating again. The wind was biting, the sky was starless, and we were five miles from the nearest exit on a remote stretch of highway. We weren't dressed for a breakdown. Our only hope for reaching a phone before frostbite set in was the neighborhood across the divided highway.

Aware of how vulnerable we were, I protectively shielded my son as we ran across the multiple lanes of speeding cars. No one stopped or even slowed down as we crossed. Since I am a sedentary woman, my son was dazzled at how fast I could run, but I was gasping for air more in fright than from exertion. Horror stories about highway breakdowns and kidnappings flitted through my mind. What kind of mother was I to put my child at risk this way? I winced to see him shiver in his thin denim jacket.

We stood there staring at an eight-foot-high security fence with no opening in the chain links, then turned to each other for inspiration. Well, I was the grown-up. I would rescue us! As I tried to wedge my size-ten tennis shoes into gaps the size of mouse holes, my hands were all that kept me off the ground. My weight bent the fence double (in the wrong direction). Hanging there upside down like a turtle on its back, I began to formulate a daring plan. Invoking the name of the Hardy Boys, I acted as if it were normal to ask your minor child to climb a fence twice his height, shred his favorite denim jacket, and vault over barbed wire to reach freedom. I broke every family rule by telling him to go to a stranger's house and ask them to phone our towing service. To my amazement, he did just that!

Can you imagine what it feels like to stand shivering and praying in pitch darkness, waiting for the sound of your young son's returning footsteps? Not good! For the first time in his life, I knew I couldn't rescue him if something happened. I like to think I would have unraveled that fence with my teeth if I'd had to, but the reality is that I was completely helpless.

I prayed, *Lord, walk every step with him. Keep him warm and bring him back to me safely.* He was gone a frighteningly long time, but then I heard him dashing through leaves calling, "Momma, are you there? Are you okay? The nice lady called for a tow truck!" Bless his heart; he was worried about me!

All parents reach a moment in time when they realize they cannot shield their children from danger. That was my moment. But in the process, I inadvertently helped my son become a hero. He amazed me by telling me how he had decided against the house with the twenty motorcycles and ear-splitting music, even though he was plenty fascinated by the bikes. My heart swelled with pride and joy, and my son walked taller as I listened to his tale. This is the stuff of which family legends are made. I suppose I should look at car problems as character-building events rather than heart-stopping, gray-hair-producing nightmares. In the end, it boils down to the sentence, "Are you okay?" Everything else is meaningless.

Dear Lord, I ask for Your protection and care over my loved ones and myself. Send Your guardian angels to protect us and lead us away from danger. Help me recognize Your intervention in my life so I will never take You for granted. Amen.

Sleepless in Pennsylvania

Carol J. Van Drie

*From the lips of children and
infants you have ordained praise.*

Psalm 8:2

When I was a young person (eons ago), my mom used to grace me with that age-old line, "Just wait till you have kids!" Yeah, sure, you know the one I mean.

As Mom predicted, I did have kids—three to be exact, and they are wonderful. But, it's true, I do see a few things more clearly from this side of childbirth. For example, if I had known then what I know now, I would have slept through a decade before conceiving in preparation for the sleep deprivation that comes automatically with motherhood. By my calculations, I haven't had a full night's sleep for almost six years.

Before I had babies, my husband (who is on active duty in the army) was stationed at Fort Lewis, Washington. I awoke one spring morning to find ash falling from the sky. I thought at first that it was dirty snow! It turned out I had actually slept through the eruption of Mount Saint Helens. The news reports said the sonic booms equaled that of several atomic bombs.

As a mom, however, I have learned that deep sleep, sleeping in, and sleeping through till morning are clearly the delicious pleasures of a bygone era. These days, my children can clear their throats in the middle of the night and I bolt upright in bed, frantically struggling with the question, *Should I get the cough medicine now or wait until they really start coughing?*

Light sleep is now the only form with which I am familiar, but if per chance I do manage to lapse into a normal sleep due to sheer exhaustion, one or more of my sweet loves will nip that unhealthy practice in the bud. That naturally will be the night they each wake up with "bad dweems" or need a "dwink" or my oldest gets the urge to discuss the upcoming elections at 1:00 A.M. I am very certain that my kids plot this type of torture when they feel that badgering the family pets hasn't given them enough satisfaction.

The other night, my husband and I found ourselves awake past midnight—an odd occurrence in our home, to say the least. There we were, watching TV—coherent and everything. I paused for a moment, gripped by the feeling that something was wrong. Then it came to me. Not once had any of our little angels gotten out of bed with a request. Of course! We were awake for crying out loud!

"Our children are unusually bright," I said to my husband. "They know instinctively that it's no challenge to bother us when we're awake. It's much more fun to yank us from the depths of dreamland!"

I guess my mom had it right all along. Being a parent is something you just can't appreciate until you are one. Kids are capable of pulling out of us a level of sacrifice and commitment that we could never have imagined before. Remember: I slept through Mount Saint Helens, but now I'm "Sleepless in Pennsylvania." And I wouldn't have it any other way!

Dear Lord, thanks for all the little lambs You have put into my life. Help me to be a good example to them. Protect them and give them opportunities to discover Your love for them. Thank You for trusting me with their care. Help me to do a good job. Amen.

In God's Hands

LaMarilys W. Doering

This is what the LORD says—your
Redeemer, who formed you in the womb:
I am the LORD, who has made all things,
who alone stretched out the heavens,
who spread out the earth by myself.

Isaiah 44:24

I had just come home from working the night shift when I crawled into my bed and pulled up the covers. Just as my eyelids were beginning to close, the phone rang. My friend Carla was on the other end, gasping for breath.

"I'm pregnant!"

I squealed with excitement. Carla had always wanted to be a mother, but now her sobs broke between her words. "But Joe wants me to abort our baby!"

Carla was almost thirty when she married. Her husband, Joe, was a gambler. He had one goal in life: to make his fortune through "lady luck." At times there was much success, and they lived high on the hog. At other times, it was only Carla's job that put bread on the table.

Carla continued, "Joe says the baby will interfere with his lifestyle. He says he wants to be a father, but we should wait till he makes the 'big one.'"

I was terrified. Abortion was not legal in those days, and Carla would have to drive to Tijuana. I feared for her life as well as the baby's. Quickly, I drove to their apartment, praying all the way. *God, it is in Your hands. Give me the words to save these lives.*

I found Carla, sitting on the sofa, deep in despair, while Joe hid himself in the bedroom. Carla said, "He won't listen."

Softly, I tapped on the bedroom door, then stepped in.

"Joe," I said softly, "Why do you want to abort your child?"

Joe's back stiffened as he turned from the dresser, tears rolling down his cheeks. "I'm no good! I love Carla and know I should be more responsible, but how? All I know is the hustle at the pool table."

Joe confided to me that he had grown up in an unstable family. Even now, he lived with the constant fear of being poor. "I'm really afraid that I won't be able to provide for my child," he said.

Having verbalized his fears, Joe stepped into the living room and took Carla into his arms. "I'm sorry. I want our baby. I'll do my level best to be a good father," he whispered.

I smiled and thanked God as they embraced.

A few months later, Carla and Joe were blessed with a beautiful baby girl. She is her daddy's pride and joy.

Joe found employment and began to climb up the corporate ladder. Not only did he turn his life around, but he became a good and loving husband and father. Just two years later, God blessed them with a precious son.

As Joe and Carla discovered, in God's hands, life can be a joy that fear cannot destroy.

Dear Lord, thank You for my life. You created me and put me into my mother's womb. I was Your idea! Help me to use this gift of life You have given me in such a way that I will be a blessing. Amen.

Oh to Be Wrinkle Free

Linda Evans Shepherd

*Jesus Christ is the same yesterday
and today and forever.*

Hebrews 13:8

Four-year-old Jimmy, smelling of blueberry glycerin soap after his evening bath, climbed into my lap with his favorite storybook. We nestled together in our big rocker.

Before I opened the book, I ran my fingers through my son's damp hair. "Did you know Daddy used to be a little boy like you?"

Jimmy looked up at me, skepticism twinkling in his eyes. "No, Mommy," he laughed. "That can't be true. You're teasing me."

"It is true!" I assured him. "Everyone, even grown-ups, used to be kids once."

Still, Jimmy looked doubtful. "Even Grandmop?"

"Yep," I answered. "Did you know Daddy's mommy was . . . is . . . Grandmop?" I asked. I gave my son a bear hug and rocked our chair back and forth. "And she used to rock Daddy in her lap just like I'm rocking you."

Jimmy's eyes widened, and he turned to look back at me. "Grandmop is Daddy's mommy?" he asked, his voice incredulous.

"That's right," I said with a smile. My eyes misted. "And someday, you are going to grow up to be big and tall, just like your daddy!"

"I will?"

I gave him a little tickle, and he giggled. "You'll be so big, I won't be able to pull you into my lap anymore."

Jimmy's giggling quieted and he said, "But Mommy, I'll always want to sit in your lap!"

I smiled. "Can you imagine Daddy trying to sit in Grandmop's lap? Why he's so big that he'd squash her!"

Jimmy threw his arms around my neck. "But, Mommy I want things to always stay the same."

I sighed. "They won't. Nothing stays the same; things are always changing. Someday, you will be a big man like Daddy, *and* you might have a little boy to snuggle in your lap, *and* I will have gray hair and lots of wrinkles."

Jimmy stopped and studied me seriously. "But, Mommy" he assured me, "you already have wrinkles!"

I had to laugh, even though my mirth only deepened my laugh lines.

Although God never promised a wrinkle-free life, He did promise us hope and a future. And that's what my young son discovered that night—that he had hope and a future, the hope that he will grow up and perhaps have a little boy of his own someday.

It's hard to realize my precious little ones will one day be too big to snuggle with me in my rocking chair. Yet, it's comforting to know I will never grow too big to crawl into my heavenly Father's lap, wrinkles and all, and rest in His love, regardless of the changes raging around me.

Dear Lord, You are the same yesterday, today, and tomorrow. No matter how my circumstances may change, You are with me. When my life shifts from one season to the next, I can still call on You and You will answer me! Amen.

The Last Great Tea Party

Patricia Lorenz

*My son, if your heart is wise,
then my heart will be glad.*

Proverbs 23:15

Andrew and I awoke to one of the coldest January days ever recorded in Milwaukee. The actual temperature was twenty-two degrees below zero, with a wind chill factor of seventy below. Most schools in southeastern Wisconsin were closed because the risk of frostbite was too great for children waiting for school buses.

We'd run out of wood for the wood burner during an earlier cold snap, and the furnace was running almost constantly. The house was still cold. I was wearing two pairs of pants, a turtleneck, and a pullover sweater, and was still shivering in the kitchen as I wondered what

Andrew, my youngest child (the only one still living at home) would do stuck in the house all day.

Just then my almost-six-foot-tall eighth grader walked into the kitchen. As I rubbed my arms to ward off a chill, Andrew asked in a perfect British accent, "Say, Mum, don't you think it's 'bout time for a spot of tea?"

I laughed as I grabbed the tea kettle to fill it with water, remembering that Andrew was in drama class that semester and that he was fascinated with his Scotch, Irish, English, French, German, and Bavarian ancestry, especially the different accents of each language. I looked closely at my son, whose father had died five years earlier, and was filled with awe at what a warm and easy relationship Andrew and I had developed over the years.

"Why certainly, my good man," I declared with as much drama as I could muster.

Andrew's eyes twinkled. He knew the scene was set. From that moment neither of us spoke in our real voices. My British accent was muddled, but I tried hard to mimic the drama in Andrew's more perfected version. From that moment on, we both became 100 percent English subjects.

"Do you fancy a spot of Earl Grey or Jasmine? English or Irish Breakfast? Blueberry, perhaps? What flavor grabs your fancy this brisk morning?"

"Say, Mum, I've always wondered. What is the difference between high tea and low tea?"

"Well, lad, low tea, which is usually called afternoon tea, is generally served at a low coffee or end table while the guests relax on a sofa or parlor chairs. High tea, is served at a high dining-room table in the early evening, our traditional supper hour. More substantial foods are served at high tea, you see." As a woman who had never had a cup of coffee in her life but who was a fanatical tea drinker, I was enjoying this opportunity to draw my son into my wonderful world of tea drinking.

Andrew rubbed his hands together as if warming them over an old English kitchen fireplace. "So, Mum, perhaps we should have a low tea on the coffee table in the living room. I'll make the preparations while you put the kettle on."

"Here, the tray is ready. Gleaming, don't you think?" I proclaimed proudly. He smiled as a glint of his true English heritage shone through his eyes, and his face was mirrored in the silver. I carefully arranged the sandwiches on the tray.

"What can we put in these tall fancy glasses, Mum?" my son quizzed as he dusted the cut glass champagne glasses that had hardly ever been used.

"A lovely fruit compote, don't you think? Here, slice this banana, and I'll cut up an apple. We'll add kiwi, raspberries, and fruit juice. It'll be fit for the Queen Mother herself," I beamed.

As we waited for the water to reheat, Andrew dashed off to his room, where he scoured his childhood collection of 160 hats, hanging on all four walls, for a proper hat to wear to what was certainly going to be a very proper low tea.

My handsome son emerged wearing an all-wool, green, yellow, and white plaid tam with a snap-down front and a bright yellow pom-pom of clipped yarn on top. My godparents, Uncle Bob and Aunt Bernadine, had given it to Andrew after a trip they took to Scotland and England. Andrew had also slipped into an old, floppy, green herringbone sport coat I'd picked up at Goodwill to wear in my workroom on cold days. I stood back and looked at my son. The hat and jacket had transformed his tall, trim body into a gentleman as striking as an English lord.

"Mum, don't you suppose you need a proper hat and skirt for the occasion?" he winked at me and shooed me off to my bedroom to change.

I headed for my own five-piece hat collection and emerged with a simple beige, wide-brimmed straw hat with a single feather protruding off to the side. To my cranberry-colored sweater, I attached an antique round pin with multi-colored stones that had belonged to Andrew's great-grandmother. A long, black, matronly skirt pulled on over my pants completed my outfit.

We were the perfect lord and lady. The tea kettle whistled. As I poured the water into the proper teapot and added loose Earl Grey tea encased in a large chrome tea ball, Andrew tuned the radio to an FM station playing classical music. He offered me his arm as we entered the living room.

As we made ourselves comfortable on the sofa, I wondered if getting ready for our tea party wasn't more fun than the actual event would be. I remembered, as a child, spending hours building a playhouse out of an enormous refrigerator-sized cardboard box. When completed—cut, colored, and decorated—the fun was over.

But I needn't have worried. As Andrew escorted me from the kitchen into the living room, where everything was picture perfect, we began an hour-and-a-half-long visit with each other that was as delightful as it was surprising.

By now, my character in our English play acting had evolved into a sort of beloved great aunt who lived in a castle, high on a hill in the English countryside and was absolutely delighted that her young nephew had dropped in for an unexpected visit. Suddenly, I wanted to know everything about this young man as I watched him carefully pour tea into the hardly-ever-used, beautiful teacups.

"So, tell me, Sir Andrew, what are your plans? Where are you going in this great adventure of life?"

Andrew leaned back on the throw pillows behind us as he sipped his Earl Grey and stroked his chin. "Well, it's a long road, you know. I still have four years of high school after this year, then college. Sometimes I wonder how I'll ever afford to attend college."

I reminded him that financial aid would be available just as it had been for his older sisters and brother. We talked about how he might get into one of his dream schools if he kept up his grades.

We slid into a conversation about girls. Andrew looked out the floor-to-ceiling windows into the barren tree tops and said slowly, "The girls. I think they all think I'm a geek."

"Oh, surely not! Why, Andrew, my good man, you're handsome, smart, funny. I bet the girls love you. You just don't know it yet."

Andrew continued to look out over the trees as he sipped the steaming tea. Then he turned and said, "I don't fight much, so they probably say I'm a wimp."

My eyes rested on Andrew's size-thirteen feet, which proclaimed that his six-foot growth spurt was not over. I reassured him that not fighting was much more manly, something the high school girls would certainly appreciate.

As time passed, we talked about music, sports, weather, God, and the school mixer coming up the next week. We watched a squirrel on the deck outside the window eating corn off a cob.

As the minutes ticked by, I felt myself opening up to the sensitive young man before me. I told Andrew how scared I had been the year before, when I quit my regular job to start a business in my home. I told him I was lonely sometimes. "You know, it's hard being here alone all day in this big old house. I miss Jeanne, Julia, and Michael. All grown. All in college. Can you believe it, Andrew?"

He nodded, poured a tiny bit of skim milk into his tea, and picked up another tea sandwich. I took a deep breath and continued, "Someday I'd love to meet a wonderful, interesting man with a great sense of humor and deep faith." I looked into the eyes of my son, who was pretending to be my grown-up nephew in drafty old England and said, "I'd like to get married again someday, Andrew. I don't want to grow old alone."

The cold morning turned warm and wonderful as we each took turns talking and listening intently to what the other had to say. We both revealed parts of ourselves that had been neglected. Every so often Andrew poured more tea for each of us. As he picked up the tiny sugar tongs he'd ask, "One lump or two, Mum?" Then he'd politely offer the plate of tiny sandwiches.

On that cold winter day, when I was forty-eight and Andrew fourteen, we were transported into a world we both knew would exist only for that one morning. I knew that when the next day came and school reopened, we would never again have a tea party like this one. Andrew would immerse himself in school, the basketball team, the junior-high band, his friends, the school play, the telephone, and video games at his best friend's house.

But it didn't matter, because on that coldest day of the year, during those precious three hours as we stumbled through a mumble jumble of British phrases and inadequate-but-charming accents, my youngest child and I ate, drank, talked, shared, laughed, and warmed our souls to the very core.

Andrew and I not only created a cherished memory, but we wrote and directed a play at the same instant we performed it. There was no audience—just Andrew and me and two cups of very good tea.

Dear Lord, help me to create special memories with my children. When they look back at their childhoods, help them to remember the laughter, not the tears. Help them to envision the smiles, not the frowns, and help them to remember our love. Amen.

Losing Her

Sue Cameron

My soul is weary with sorrow;
strengthen me according to your word.

Psalm 119:28

She's leaving for college in just a few weeks. We've made preparations. We went to the dentist and had her teeth cleaned, bought contacts, made lists of things to take, cleaned out her closet, purchased tickets so she could come home at Thanksgiving. And I've been figuring out how to rearrange the furniture in her bedroom to make it into a study. A place just for me, where I can spread out with space for my files and a bookshelf for my books. After years of squeezing in here and there, sharing space, I'm dreaming of a desk of my own.

Everything seemed to be going along as planned—until today. Just before she left for work, we had a confrontation. Our voices were raised, our emotions running deep.

"I can't believe you want to put all my things in the basement. This is still my home. I live here. I'm just going away to college!"

"Honey," I reasoned, "you'll only be here for holidays."

"And all summer!" She tossed her head and I caught that look in her eye. It said, *I'm really looking forward to this, Mom, but I'm scared, too. I want to leave and grow up, but don't you want to beg me to stay?* Last night, she had curled up next to me on the couch. "Scratch my head," she purred. "Now my back. You won't get to do this much longer."

Her declarations of independence tinged with her pleas for pity have puzzled me. But maybe I'm beginning to hear what my little princess is telling me. She needs reassurance that life won't be quite as special once she's gone.

Perhaps she needs a place to come back to—just in case. Maybe I need to explain that her leaving is ripping a hole in my heart. When I look at her I can still see past the woman she has become and glimpse the child she was. I can recall the press of her tiny fingers as they wrapped around mine a moment after her birth. I can close my eyes and remember the scent of her fresh, new baby skin and the feel of her fuzzy head against my cheek. I can all but hear her toddler's plea of, "Mom-

mom, hold me-me." Perhaps she needs to be sure that no one could ever take her place and that I'll miss her more than she'll ever know.

Maybe she wants to see me hurt just a little and mourn losing her. Instead of my being eager to turn her room into a study, perhaps she longs for me to melt into a puddle of tears—to see the pain that tells her she is still special to me.

And maybe she's right. Instead of putting up this brave front—this shield of reorganizing the house and quickly going on with life—perhaps I need to allow the pain of this parting to sweep over me. Perhaps I need to taste the grief of knowing that our family is changing and will never to be the same because my little girl has grown up. Maybe I need to acknowledge that while I'm very proud of her, I also long for those days when she needed me in so many ways.

Maybe she knows more than I do—that it will be better for me in the coming months to be able to go into her familiar bedroom, bury my face in one of her stuffed polar bear's fur, and cry because my baby grew up too fast. And maybe she understands that if I pack away all her knickknacks and keepsakes, my fingers will have nothing to grasp when my arms ache to hold her.

Maybe she knows better than I do that I'm not ready for a study yet, and losing her is harder than I want to admit.

Dear Lord, our children are in our care for such a little while. It is difficult to see them grow up and walk out into life without us. Help them be prepared to face the world as they spread their wings to fly. Amen.

Friendship

Friendship happens when two hearts carry the same weight.

Anonymous

Finders Keepers

Rosey Dow

Love one another deeply, from the heart.
1 Peter 1:22

Twenty minutes before service time, I walked into church and found a seat in the third row. The other teens were milling around, talking and laughing. I was alone. I opened my Bible and pretended to read it, trying to look unconcerned. This was my second week at Capitol Baptist. I didn't know a single soul.

"Hi!" a slim girl with hip-length, black hair sidled into the next row and sat sideways in the pew so she could face me. "My name's Anna. What's yours?"

I forced my lips to curve upward and said, "Rosey." I wanted to say more, but I didn't know the words. I never did.

"We're going to Hershey Park next Saturday," Anna said. "Would you like to pal around with me?"

My smile turned into something real. "Sure. What time?"

Before dawn on Saturday, I met her by the yellow bus in the church parking lot where twenty-five teens milled about the lot, swapping insults, stealing hats, and bugging the counselors with questions. The youth director, Eddie, took their antics in stride. He was a big kid himself. Eddie had a gold front tooth in the middle of his wide smile and a giant heart that loved us all.

At Hershey Park, the young people divided into small groups. Anna and I teamed up with two other girls. The other three wanted to get on every ride that moved, especially the ones that made them scream.

Heights terrified me. I spent most of the morning waiting at exit gates.

After lunch, Anna did some fast talking. She persuaded me to get on a log ride that soaked my dress and hair. Then she laughed at me. I loved it.

After that day, Anna and I were like Siamese twins at church services, teen activities, and school. She was a sophomore, and I was a senior. The age difference meant nothing. She taught me so many things. Our personalities were poles apart, but we had two things in common: we both came from broken homes, and we both loved God.

Anna's soldier father married a Japanese lady after World War II. Like a romance novel or a movie, he brought her to America to live happily ever after. Ten years later, he abandoned his family and disappeared without a trace. Anna's mother, who spoke little English, had to provide for six children.

My mother married again less than a month after her divorce from my father. Within a month, my stepfather showed his true character. His foul mouth belittled anyone who crossed his path. He lied compulsively and used violence to keep us in fear. I lived for the day that I could escape his abuse.

Anna and I propped each other up. We shared our deepest secrets and giggled for the craziest reasons. We prayed together, cried together, and planned our futures together. We finished each other's sentences and even came to believe that we could read each other's thoughts.

At the end of the school year, Mrs. Joines, a lady in our church, asked us to "baby-sit" her eighty-year-old mother, Mrs. Dekker, while she traveled to New York on business for two days. Mrs. Dekker was afraid to be in the house alone at night.

The first night, Anna brought her teddy bear and told him outrageous things about me until I whacked her with a pillow. Then she sat yoga-style in the middle of

the bed and made weird humming noises. I grabbed her
feet and pulled her off the bed. Later, our chins
propped on our hands, we philosophized about life and
that special someone who was still a mysterious shadow
in our dreams.

A few months later, I told Anna that God had called
me to be a missionary. Our tears mingled when she
hugged me. Since I had enrolled in a local college after
graduation, we had two more years together. Then, I
transferred to a Florida college. Anna followed me a
year later. We were roommates and soulmates—again.

At college, our relationship began to change. During
my year without Anna, I had come to grips with my
bitterness against my stepfather. God had delivered me
from the anger and the pain. Anna had yet to deal with
her past. Now, instead of Anna leading me, I was in a
position to help her.

Shortly after the term began, Anna was involved in a
violation of school rules. I knew that if she apologized,
the penalty would most likely be softened, but if she
rebelled, it was possible that she would be expelled.
Chin high, she told me the incident wasn't her fault.
We locked ourselves in the bathroom away from prying
ears while I begged her to swallow her pride. We

argued, cried together, and finally prayed. Anna finished the year.

The next year I became a bride. Anna transferred to a South Carolina college, and my husband and I moved to Maryland. Later, we left America to be missionaries in the Caribbean. Eighteen years passed without a word from Anna.

When we arrived at our mission headquarters for our second furlough, someone came to me in the dining room. "Rosey, you have a call in the office." I rushed down the long hall, realizing that the call was surely long distance.

"Hello?" I panted into the receiver.

A woman's voice said, "Do you know who this is?"

I hesitated.

"It's Anna."

"Anna!" I gripped the phone like a lifeline. "Anna, where are you?"

"Kansas. My husband teaches history in a Christian school, and I teach elementary art."

Husband? I held back tears. How much we had missed.

"I want you to visit us when you're back in the States," she said.

The next spring, when we went home to visit our supporting churches, we drove two thousand miles out of our way to do just that. Time melted away the moment we saw each other. She looked exactly the same: tall and lean as a bamboo stalk, black hair tied into a ponytail, and that crooked front tooth she liked to tap with her thumb. Her two little boys bounced with excitement while my seven offspring (five of them teenagers) scrutinized Mom's old friend.

Our husbands escaped to the backyard to enjoy male small talk while Anna and I caught up on half a lifetime. Within five minutes, we were once again finishing each other's sentences.

Anna and I spent two days together, but it seemed like two hours. "I've had many acquaintances through the years, but I've never found another friend like you," Anna confided as we were leaving. "I'm praying that someday God will let us live near each other again."

She hadn't lost her touch. She could still read my mind.

Dear Lord, it is so marvelous what the touch of one human being can do to change our lives. Thank You for providing friends like that. Help me to be a friend like that to others. Amen.

A Ray of Sunshine

Cindy Heflin

*A friend loves at all times,
and a brother is born for adversity.*

Proverbs 17:17

I sat in silence by the kitchen window as another autumn morning began. The damp and dreary scene outside mirrored the heavy clouds that had covered me for weeks. Sipping a steaming cup of tea, I scanned the overcast skies, searching for a glimpse of sunshine. While my children slept, I lingered alone, deep in thought. Though I longed to feel the warmth of God's presence, my hot cup of tea did little to change the climate of my heart. I whispered a prayer asking God for help and a ray of sunshine to break through the clouds of my despair.

Though several weeks had passed, it seemed like the car accident had happened only yesterday. The ophthalmology report that followed now overshadowed my life and slammed the brakes on my independence. My doctor's painful announcement echoed in my mind, "Vision severely deteriorated . . . never drive again." It crushed me to face my visual limitations and the certainty of gradual blindness.

Suddenly the children's playful voices suspended my thoughts and signaled the start of another busy day. I muddled through a typical morning of breakfast, laundry, and Play-Doh, struggling to understand, "Why did God allow this to happen?" Although overcome with despair and anxiety, I knew He would take care of my needs, but how?

My husband frequently traveled out of town on business for days, sometimes weeks at a time. With two young daughters to care for, my days were filled with trips to the supermarket, the preschool, and the doctor's office. I enjoyed being independent and self-sufficient. I felt uncomfortable asking for help, unwilling to be a burden or to depend on others. The challenges of my new limitations overwhelmed me. Even with God's help, it seemed impossible to cope with this sudden change in my life.

The telephone rang as I collapsed onto the sofa, weary from a long afternoon. To my surprise, the friendly caller was Mary, a young mom from our church. Despite our

A RAY OF SUNSHINE

mutual friends, we had never met. With compassion, she expressed her concern for me and for my family. Gently she offered, "You know . . . I'm always out with my children. I'd really love the company if you ever need a ride."

Tears trickled down my cheeks as she suggested that she come by and pick us up one day each week to run errands! As I hung up the phone, my heart filled with amazement and gratitude. God had heard my prayer, and He had faithfully answered! After supper, baths, and bedtime stories, I kissed my girls goodnight with a new sense of peace in my heart. Exhausted, I fell into bed, thanking the Lord for His provision.

Mary arrived promptly the next afternoon. Her bright smile and cheerful nature were as sunny as the buttercup-colored sedan she drove. Each Tuesday at noon, we strapped the children into their car seats; confirmed an ample supply of diapers, toys, and snacks; and set out for an afternoon on the road. Soon, I realized traveling with Mary was more than just a trip to the post office, bank, or grocery store—it was FUN! She entertained the children with games and songs as we made our rounds "all through the town." Her joy and laughter were good medicine for my weary soul.

A day out with Mary was always delightful and optimistic, lifting my spirits with lively conversation. Discussions often centered on our faith in Christ as she encouraged me to seek Him for the strength to overcome my trials. On the difficult days, she reassured me that with God, all things are possible!

The warm breezes and welcome sunshine of spring revealed a renewed hope in my spirit. In addition to our weekly trek, Mary often invited us along to the playground, to the park for a picnic, to "Mommy and me" day at the YMCA, and even for a day trip out of town! It meant so much to me to once again enjoy these simple pleasures with my daughters! My despair diminished, and my faith grew stronger as I learned to focus on the Lord's faithfulness and compassion. During my darkest days, He sent me a cherished friend to lighten my burdens and bless me in many ways.

The Lord's faithful provision for my needs was more than I ever could have imagined. The generosity and spiritual encouragement I received from Mary and other caring friends has taught me the powerful impact of reaching out to others. This motivates me to follow their example. For I know that sharing God's hope with others is like a ray of sunshine on a cloudy day!

Dear Lord, thank You for friends.
They are like a secret garden growing in
my heart. May the seeds of our friendships
blossom into great bouquets of happiness and
carry the scent of our joy to others. Amen.

A Friend Like Marcy

Deborah Raney

He who walks with the wise grows wise.

Proverbs 13:20

The first time I met Marcy, she was bent over a conveyer, pasting address labels onto folded newspapers. Eight months pregnant, she and her husband, Kurt, had moved back to his hometown to work for the family newspaper business where I was employed as a typesetter. At first, I was a bit intimidated by this cultured (she had studied violin and piano), thin (even for being eight months pregnant!), sophisticated-looking brunette. It didn't help that she carried it off without a trace of makeup.

Perhaps the fact that Marcy was my boss's daughter-in-law kept me from seeking out her friendship. Still, I was drawn to her. We shared our experiences as newly-weds and compared notes on our pregnancies. My first son was just beginning to toddle, and I remembered well the excitement I felt as we waited for his birth.

Our friendship began to jell when I visited Marcy in the hospital after her daughter was born. Almost fearfully, I took the elevator to the maternity ward, wondering if she would see my visit as an intrusion.

Though surprised by my visit, Marcy quickly regained her composure, and we had a warm conversation as we walked down the hallway to "ooh and aah" together at the nursery window. Several weeks later, Marcy asked my husband and me to baby-sit for little Rebekah while she and Kurt went to some fancy press club dinner. I still remember the classically designed mauve suit she wore for the evening, her long, thick hair pulled back off her high forehead with a tortoise-shell barrette. But later when they came to pick up Rebekah, she kicked off her stylish shoes and barely batted an eyelash when the baby spit up on her expensive jacket. Somehow, I began to feel I really had found a new friend.

Soon we were both mothers at home, and our friendship blossomed. I quickly learned that Marcy was a spontaneous person. I came to love her phone calls. "I'm standing in a mountain of laundry," she would say. "Why don't you bring the kids over and keep me company while I fold clothes," or "Let's take the kids to the park for a picnic."

Unlike me, Marcy never worried that her house had to meet certain standards of cleanliness or her cupboards had to be stocked just so in order for company to be welcomed. At Marcy's house, peanut butter and honey sandwiches were served on paper plates with all the flourish of a gourmet meal served on fine china dishes.

I quickly learned that Marcy was an honest person. She had no qualms about telling you that, yes, that dress really does make you look fat. But, if she told you she loved your new haircut—by George—you knew she really did! More than any other friend I've known, Marcy taught me that it is possible to be loved just the way you are.

From her I also learned that the most comfortable seat in the house just might be a sofa piled high with freshly laundered diapers waiting to be folded. And the best cup of coffee might be sipped at a sticky kitchen table strewn with broken crayons and cookie crumbs.

When I discovered I was pregnant again after desperately wanting another baby for almost three years, Marcy arrived at our back door bearing a huge box of saltines and a two-liter bottle of 7-Up. We sat on the backporch steps and toasted the occasion with Tupperware sipper cups.

I was thrilled when just before our daughter was born, Marcy announced that she, too, was expecting her second child. I traded my maternity clothes for her baby clothes, and nine months later, when Kurt dropped two-year-old Rebekah off at our house early one morning, I waited anxiously for the news of the new baby's safe arrival.

Photographs taken two years later at a baby shower for my new little son, Trey, show Marcy eating cake and sipping punch and wearing "my" favorite maternity dress—one she had sewn for her first pregnancy.

Soon she had two girls and a boy, I had two boys and a girl, and life got incredibly hectic. Still, Marcy always made it a point to find ways to connect. For a time, she helped out with the family newspaper business by making deliveries to a small town nearby. Many Thursday mornings my phone would ring, and soon, two young moms, six toddlers in tow, would be piling into the company van for the twenty-mile trip and the sheer joy of shared company. We cherished as many minutes of adult conversation as we could sandwich between diaper changes and toddler skirmishes. Sometimes she had to pull over to the side of the road because I was nursing my baby and—well, six babies were simply more than either of us could handle with one free hand.

As our kids grew, we compared notes on everything from potty training to discipline to spiritual philosophies. We didn't always agree, but we never lost the deep respect we had for one another.

When my husband was laid off and his new job made a move imminent, I didn't let myself think about how much I would miss Marcy. Her fourth baby, John Kurtis, was born on May 21, and ten days later we pulled out of our driveway for the last time. It made me sad to think that I would not get to know this little boy the way I had grown to know and love his mother and siblings.

But our move was within the state, and Marcy and I soon found a Hardee's Restaurant almost exactly halfway between us. I still remember the anticipation of those early-morning, fifty-mile drives to share coffee and a cinnamon roll with a precious friend.

One awful year, my phone rang a few weeks before Christmas. It was Kurt calling to tell me that Marcy was in the hospital. The doctors had found cancer. It was something I had silently feared, given her mother's history. But now, I couldn't believe it was really happening. There was surgery and radiation. I wanted to pack my bags to go and stay with her for as long as she needed help. But of course, that was impossible. My family needed me, too.

I was privileged to occasionally drive with her to doctor's appointments in a nearby city, and we would have long reflective conversations over lunch afterward. We prayed for each other often.

When Marcy's husband took a job in Ohio, the good-byes were harder. She came to see me before the move, and we pretended not to know this might be the last visit for a long while—maybe forever. But when we gave each other that last hug, we both cried—big gulping sobs accompanied by very unladylike nose blowing.

Ten years have passed since that good-bye. From all appearances, Marcy's cancer is gone. For me, it's no longer anything more than a few scary days each year waiting for the tests and that wonderful phone call that says, "Everything looks fine; all the tests were negative." For her, I'm sure there are still some unspoken, nagging worries. But Marcy never has been one to let a little thing like cancer get her down.

My husband and I had another daughter nine years ago. Now Marcy and I each have two sons and two daughters. Seven of our eight combined children are in high school or college now. Marcy and I still get together, but our conversations are about curfews and dating and college exams instead of potty-training and breast-feeding. I can hardly believe we've known each other long enough for this thing called "growing up" to have happened to our children!

Marcy lives several hours away now, and we keep in touch with long, newsy, much-too-infrequent letters and e-mails. Our visits are too few and far between. But some things never change. Every time we do get together, whether it's been two months or two years, it's the same. We reintroduce the kids to one another, get out the coffeepot, and catch up on all the mundane, little details of each other's lives. Then Marcy and I leave the husbands in charge, and the two of us set out on a long walk. As the years fall away, we remember together where we've been, and we rejoice in where life may take us. We celebrate the friendship that binds us together for a lifetime.

Dear Lord, it is so hard when life's journey separates me from a friend. Please go with her and comfort her heart. Let her know that I am with her no matter how many miles may separate us. Thank You for the kind of friendship that lasts a lifetime. Amen.

The Friendship Quilt

Heidi Hess Saxton

Do not forsake your friend.

Proverbs 27:10

"If you want to go look at her quilt patterns, fine. But I don't have time this week for silly blankets." The look on her face told me instantly that I had wounded her as only friends can wound one another. Embarrassed, I tried to make excuses. I was under pressure; I'd hardly had five minutes to call my own that week. Still, I knew I had blown it. In two seconds, I had managed to unravel a gaping hole in our friendship.

It was a small thing, really. Diane, one of Jane's oldest and dearest friends, was in town. She had invited Jane to tea and an afternoon of quilting, and Jane wanted me to go along and get to know Diane better. But the awful truth was, I didn't want to know her better. I didn't like what I knew of Diane already. She was far too outspoken, far too superior, and far too irritating.

As far as I could tell, Diane and Jane had only one thing in common—quilting. And I had no interest in pricking my fingers all afternoon, just waiting for Diane to say something else that would get my knickers in a knot. So I brushed aside Jane's invitation, trying not to notice the hurt in her eyes. "Well," she said softly, "if you change your mind, here's where I'll be." She wrote down an address and handed it to me.

All afternoon I had a lemon-sized knot in the pit of my stomach. Finally I got in my car, drove to the address Jane had given me, and rang the doorbell. Jane's eyes lit up when I walked into the room. "Oh, I'm so glad you could join us! Come and help us pick out the colors," she said. "We're making a friendship quilt!"

Fingering the gingham and flowered fabrics, I noticed the knot in my stomach disappear. Diane held up two swatches and asked for my opinion, then nodded her approval of my choice. The afternoon flew by. And the tapestry of friendship was magically restored.

Dear Lord, thank You for stitching friends into the fabric of my life. Their colorful patterns and personalities add a richness and texture to who I am. May we provide loving comfort to one another as we walk along life's path. Amen.

Turning the Page

Jan Coleman

*Dear friend, I pray that you may enjoy good
health and that all may go well with you,
even as your soul is getting along well.*

3 John 2

Jeanne first appeared on moving day, sometime after
the last box was unloaded. With brownies in hand, she
welcomed me to the neighborhood. She had sunshine in
her steps, and it lifted my heart right away.

Recently single again, I was forced to give up my
country dream home for a small duplex in town, and my
spirits were as high as the grass in the front yard. I hated
the word "single." Once it was only a name for slices of
cheese or the 45-RPM records I played as a teenager.
Now, it was a summary of my miserable condition.

Yet, Jeanne wore singleness well. Right away she got
me out hiking and mountain biking. We shared the

same passion for old movies, historical novels, and Scrabble games.

With each year that went by, I laughed more and pondered my past hurts less. Jeanne became the sister I never had. Singleness wasn't so bad after all. My daughters were healing and stopped rebelling. I had a challenging job and an active social life. Jeanne and I joined the leadership team of a singles' ministry, planning programs and writing humorous skits to teach singles how to laugh at themselves. We made a great team, and God used our pain and failures to encourage others.

Life couldn't have been better.

A few years later, Jeanne was offered a six-month teaching exchange in New Zealand that she could not pass up. I didn't know what to do with myself—but not for long.

Carl started inviting me for coffee after the singles' meetings. I never intended to grow in deeper friendship with him, but my years with Jeanne had opened my wounded heart to trust again. By the time I met her plane in San Francisco, it was clear that Carl was the mate God intended for me. My decade of singleness was coming to an end.

I prayed for a partner for Jeanne. "Please Lord, can't we transition into couplehood together?"

Though Mr. Right never surfaced, Jeanne still relished every detail of my courtship. Yet we avoided talking about splitting up the team. For the first time, we were at a loss for words.

The weekend before my wedding, Jeanne kidnapped me and took me to a cabin in Tahoe, our last outing as single sisters. As we sat in front of a roaring fire, gazing at snowcapped peaks, the jumbled emotions came gushing out.

We felt like Siamese twins, facing the loss of our second selves, uncertain how our friendship would have to change. There would be no more 5:00 A.M. phone calls from Jeanne, no more popping over in her pajamas for movie night or leaving me a message, "It's payback time. Set up the Scrabble board when you get home from work." My focus would be on building a marriage; Jeanne would form a new circle of friends and activities.

This chapter of our lives was coming to a close, and we had to grieve. In all the years I yearned for remarriage, who would have thought it would come with an ache like this? How odd that a part of my past I once scorned was now so cherished, all because God brought a friend into my life.

But every page must turn or the story can't continue.

On my wedding eve, after writing my vows, I penned a letter to Jeanne. I cried as I recounted all our antics together, the way she buoyed me up with her cheerfulness, how she will always have a special place in my heart that no one else can fill, not even Carl.

After my marriage, she gave me space to adjust to my new role by taking a leave of absence for missionary training. After living in the Philippines, Jeanne had new priorities and vision for her future. Her enthusiasm for the Lord inspired Carl and me to try a ministry at church we could do together.

It's been five years since Jeanne and I broke up our act, but we still make time for just the two of us, especially when we need a Scrabble fix. Tonight, she'll bound through the door in her sweats and get a big hug from Carl. He'll grin at us before slipping quietly into his office. I'll set up the board while Jeanne slips her feet snugly into her cozy slippers and brews herself a cup of tea.

It could be a long night.

Dear Lord, help me not to disconnect from those You have placed in my life. I may make new friends, but an old friend cannot be replaced. Help me to cherish the friends You have given me. Amen.

Laughter

Joy is the echo of God's life within us.

Joseph Marmion

Short(s)
Circuited

Patsy Clairmont

She is clothed with strength and dignity;
she can laugh at the days to come.

Proverbs 31:25

Knowing my friend Nancy is like embracing a waterfall. She splashes over with energy, excitement, and enthusiasm for life and people. She's filled with joy and also mischievousness. Her mind and wit are quick and memorable. David, her husband, is a courageous man who has survived and been blessed by Nancy's outrageous humor. We all remember when. . . .

David is mellow and usually cooperates and enjoys his wife's wishes and whims. But one day the two of them had a tiff, and neither Nancy nor David would budge from the feeling of being in the right. Several days had passed since the difference between them arose, and static hung in the air, droning out communication.

David would normally give in under such circumstances, but not this time. Nancy was amazed he wasn't talking, but she was equally determined not to speak first.

Then it happened. David came home and started to pack his suitcase. Nancy was confident he wasn't leaving her; he was often sent on business trips. But she couldn't believe he would go without resolving their conflict first. David, however, jaw set, silently prepared to leave. Nancy fumed.

Most of us, when we fume, have to verbally spew so we don't become combustible and explode. Not Nancy. She uses her hostility to create . . . well, let's just say, memories.

That night, they went to bed without a word. David was feeling a slight advantage in their "cold war," because he knew what his travel plan was, and she didn't. He also knew this would bug her, because she's a detail person and likes to be fully informed. David fell asleep that night with a smirk on his face. I don't think he would have rested as well as he did, however, had he seen the grin spreading across his stalemate's lips.

David rose the next morning and went in to take his shower. While he was washing up, Nancy was quietly yukking it up. First, she counted his undershorts in the suitcase to see how many days he would be gone. Finding that out, she then could determine where he was going. He always went to one of two places, each requiring him to stay a different length of time.

Once she figured out his destination, she quickly lifted the neatly folded underwear out of his luggage and replaced it with a note. Stifling giggles, she stashed his confiscated shorts in a drawer, zipped his case closed, dashed back between the bedsheets, and used a pillow to muffle her pleasure.

David emerged showered and shaved, picked up his suitcase, and left for his trip. This was the first time they had parted company without hugs, kisses, and promises to call. They were both finding a bit of comfort, though, in thinking they had a secret the other didn't know.

The outbound flight put David in a confined place with time to think. He began to feel bad about their stormy week and his stony departure. He dearly loved Nancy and promised himself and the Lord that he would call and apologize as soon as he arrived at his hotel.

Nancy, in the meantime, busied herself around the house, stopping occasionally to imagine David's reaction when he unpacked. Chuckling, she waited for the phone to ring, both dreading and delighting in the prospect.

She didn't have long to wait. "Mom, it's Dad; he wants to talk to you," her son yelled.

Nancy wasn't sure if she should run to the phone or run for cover. But she made her way to the table and picked up the receiver. What she heard was not what she had anticipated. On the other end, David confessed his regrets at their spat and expressed even greater sorrow at leaving without making things right.

Nancy's heart sank as she was warmed by his tenderness and sincerity. She decided she had better fess up, too.

"David, have you unpacked yet?" she inquired.

"No, not yet."

"Maybe you should," she suggested.

"Why, what did you do?"

"Just go open your suitcase; I'll wait on the line."

David came back chuckling. "Very funny, Nancy. Where did you put my shorts?"

"Oh, they're here in the drawer," she admitted.

"No, really, are they in a side pocket?"

"Honest, I took them out before you left. Isn't that funny, David?" she said with failing confidence.

The line was silent, and then, much to her delight, David broke into gales of healing laughter.

The note? Oh, yeah, it read: "David, your attitude stinks and now so does your only pair of underwear!"

Dear Lord, if my attitude smells to high heaven, help me to trash my complaints and bitterness. Replace this garbage with Your love so my attitude will be a delight to both You and to those around me. Amen.

Do You Know Where Your Children Are?

Connie Bertelsen Young

A time to laugh.

Ecclesiastes 3:4

I was a family day-care provider in the '80s, and I treated the children who were in my care like they were my own. In fact, I still have a habit of calling them "mine," although they were "mine" for only a few hours each week.

The other day, my cousin and I visited a friend in the hospital. As we were getting on the elevator, I noticed the parent of a child who was in my day care. I really put my foot in my mouth when I introduced him to my cousin very matter-of-factly: "This is the father of one of my eighteen children."

The people standing around us in the crowded elevator gave me some horrified looks (my cousin later informed me), but at the time, I was oblivious to the implications of my statement. And unfortunately, that wasn't the end of it.

The father, among the horrified, failed to recognize me, although he feebly attempted to respond to me since I had spoken his name, so I blundered on in all seriousness. "You probably don't remember me, but I believe you're the father of one of my kids."

Once I comprehended the enormity of what I'd said, my embarrassment temporarily put me at a loss for words, and his obvious, mortified response made it even harder for me to get myself together.

After seconds of uncomfortable silence while the elevator descended to the ground floor, my cousin fell into rather loud hysterics. Distracted by her demented laughter, I didn't use the brief opportunity I had to elaborate before the dumbfounded man rushed out of the elevator.

I'm comforted knowing that we were not far from an emergency room, just in case he couldn't recover himself. But what had I done? Will that man think for the rest of his life that he somehow fathered a child he knows nothing about?

Sir, just in case you are reading this, let me assure you that you don't owe me any back child support. Also, for the sake of my own reputation, let it be known that I have just two children, both of whom know their father very well.

Dear Lord, help me to see the humor in life. Thank You for giggles and smiles. Help me to use them effectively as I sprinkle them through my day. May I see the joy in all my circumstances. Amen.

Naked Glamour

Lynda Munfrada

Nothing in all creation is hidden from God's sight Everything is uncovered and laid bare before the eyes of him to whom we must give account.

Hebrews 4:13

It wasn't bad enough that I had already spilled my grape juice on the fine restaurant table linens (white, of course) or almost tossed our gorgeous guest speaker right into the salad bowl when I broke the heel off one of my new black dress shoes. Oh, no, God had laughter in mind when He made me. And I love Him for it!

For one year I had faithfully attended a Christian women's group and had finally mustered up the courage to help decorate for the next luncheon. It was to be held at a prestigious banquet room, and I was in charge of the centerpieces. The theme was "Glamorous Gals for God." I blushed with honor as they explained that I would even get to sit at the head table, two seats down from the famous guest speaker, an actress and author of many fine books on charm and elegance. Excitement gushed forth like the fountain of Florentine.

"You've got to be kidding!" I cried into the receiver as I stared into the newly delivered box of "straw."

Jan, the women's group coordinator, gleefully cheered through the phone, "Oh, good! You've got the centerpieces!"

"They're, they're—" I searched for an appropriate yet non-offensive word, "Barbie dolls! And they're—naked!"

"I know!" she exuded. "Aren't they bee-u-tee-ful?"

They're Barbies, and they're naked! How could I tell her that I didn't like Barbie dolls, never had one as a child, and never ever thought they were bee-u-tee-ful?

"Is there a problem with them?" Jan's voice quivered at my silence.

I didn't want to seem incompetent or offend my new friend, but I knew my heart wasn't going to be in this. My enthusiasm drizzled into sludge.

"No," I weakly smiled. "They'll work." I prayed and did the best I could.

Two weeks later, I had polished, coifed, and gowned thirty-seven "bee-u-tees" in hand-sewn and crocheted, beaded, glittered, and jeweled gowns. One doll was even bedecked in a miniature Doris Day pink satin replica. The gown was form fitted, slit up the side, and included a miniature mink jacket made from a scrap of my great-grandmother's old tattered stole. "Doris," as I affectionately called her, was carefully placed on the left side of the head of the table in front of the guest speaker's place card.

"Marilyn," at the other end, stood just as proud in her brilliant red billowing halter-top dress. The promise of an elegant afternoon loomed before me. Even I began to feel a little gorgeous in my homemade Joan Crawford-type black and ivory dinner dress. I almost relaxed. Almost.

One little task remained. Sandwiched in between Jan's announcements and the guest speaker's monologue, I was to take a bow for the centerpieces and give a brief history or inspirational note about each one. Nervousness and excitement blended with three glasses of ice tea, and, just before my oration, I was in dire need of a bathroom break. When Jan approached the podium, I made my move to the back of the room, down the hall, and into privacy to quiet my nerves. Not wanting to sound prideful for the praise-worthy job I had done, I practiced words of humility to lavish upon my adoring fans in the bathroom mirror. I hurried back to the room and began a walk that I will never forget.

As I passed the rows of tables, two on the left, two on the right, each adorned with a mini masterpiece, silence followed. The usual murmur that permeates the back of a room during a speech, eerily stopped as if I were dragging a veil of death behind me as I walked to my place at the head table. I sat down just as Jan introduced me. As I stood to deliver the great, yet humble speech about the gorgeous gowns, the guest speaker leaned and whispered into my ear.

"Your skirt hem is caught in the back of your pantyhose."

Realizing my exposure, I hurriedly sat back down and adjusted all the necessary items, including my pride. As red as Marilyn's dress, I slowly faced the sea of wide-eyed spectators. I drew in a deep breath of honest humility and calmly offered, "Well, now that some of my best work has been revealed, let's look at the rest of the clothing." Five minutes of tidal-wave laughter later, I began my commentary in true modesty.

When I get prideful and look only on the outward appearance, God reminds me that I'm not a finished product, and I must rely on His goodness and glory to be "clothed . . . with garments of salvation and arrayed . . . in a robe of righteousness" (Isaiah 61:10). When I am thus attired, I am well dressed indeed.

Dear Lord, help me to accessorize every outfit with a smile. Give me contentment even when there are holes in my socks and my stretch pants have no other choice. Even then, I know I will be dressed for success, for my attitude will outshine any fashion statement my neighbor can afford. Amen.

I Was Dressed to Impress

Nancy Kennedy

*You turned my wailing into
dancing; you removed my sackcloth
and clothed me with joy.*

Psalm 30:11

One morning, as I stared into my jam-packed closet, I realized I had nothing to wear to an upcoming lunch interview with a potential employer, so I called a friend for advice.

"Maria, I need you to help me pick out something strong and dignified for my meeting," I pleaded. "Or at least something presentable that I can still get into!"

Maria came right over and joined me in staring into the closet, "Nancy," she said as she held up outfit after outfit, "no offense. You have a lot of stuff here, but you can't wear any of it to your meeting."

She started pitching my favorite outfits into one huge reject pile: my "If I Only Had a Brain" sweatshirt, my neon pink turtleneck with matching bolero pants, even my faux-fur-collared, brown, imitation-vinyl ski jacket. She tossed until nothing was left.

"Anything else wrong with my clothes?" I asked, watching one lone coat hanger wobble on the bar.

"Nancy, didn't anyone tell you that you can't wear peach?"

I looked over the pile of clothes on the floor, half of them peach. "Why can't I?"

"Because you're obviously a 'summer,' and summers don't wear peach."

"Okay," I said. "Can I wear black?"

"Uh-uh."

"Cream or beige?"

She made a gagging gesture that I took to mean no. "What's left?" I asked.

"Light pink and any shade of blue."

I picked up a bright-yellow blouse and held it up to my face. "Maria, are you sure?"

"Trust me," she said.

Back before shopping became a science, I liked going to the mall. I could people watch, get some exercise, and most importantly, buy anything in any color I wanted. But then I went shopping with Maria, and suddenly it felt more like a military mission than something fun.

Maria called our mission "Dress to Impress," and our motto was, "If it doesn't scream 'power,' put it back." Together we looked for something simple and conservative and finally decided on a straight, navy blue skirt and a pink jacket with navy window-pane checks. Underneath the jacket went a white silk blouse, underneath that a camisole and a pair of shoulder pads. Because I've had a couple of kids and still have what my husband affectionately refers to as "abdominal overhang," Maria shoved me into some stomach-restricting foundations. I couldn't breathe and sit at the same time—but at least I could button my jacket.

Next my outfit needed shoes—high heels. I'll spare you my feeling on those. Let's just say I know they were designed by a podiatrist who needed some extra business. However, Maria assured me they were non-negotiable. "You can't show up wearing your Reeboks or those horrible open-toed brown things of yours," she warned.

After the shoes and matching clutch bag, we completed my outfit with a chain, earrings, and a scarf to drape over my left shoulder. I'd just spent almost my entire year's clothing budget on one "power outfit" that squashed my stomach and pinched my toes. I guess that's what power does to a person.

The morning of my lunch meeting, I have to admit that as I got dressed, power surged through my jacketed body. I was going to march into that restaurant dressed to impress and bowl over my prospective employer.

March I did—right out of the car and into a puddle. I wobbled into the restaurant and into the ladies' room to wash off my stockings and shoes. In the process, I got my new scarf wet and the colors (navy, pink, and turquoise) bled onto the left side of my jacket.

I thought I could get away with removing my jacket and wearing just the skirt and blouse. But that's when I discovered that silk makes me sweat, and since wearing sweat-soaked white silk is a lot like wearing nothing at all, I had no choice but to keep my jacket on and stay turned to the right.

Already ten minutes late, I wobbled on my squishy heels into the dining area to meet the woman who held my future in her hands. I took a step toward her and, in an attempt to stay turned to the right, caught my heel on the edge of my chair and tripped before I caught myself on a nearby table.

It's true—your whole life passes before your eyes when you're dying, and dying of embarrassment is no exception. I stumbled for only a few seconds, but it seemed like hours from my vantage point. I saw I had only two choices. Run out of there and never show my face in public again (especially at that restaurant), or introduce myself and laugh it off.

"A simple curtsy will do," my lunch companion said, helping me regain my balance. She grinned and for a moment, I sensed everything would be all right. That is until I discovered that shoulder pads shift to unusual places if not firmly anchored in place.

I took a breath, then smiled as if this were an everyday occurrence. "How do you do?" I said, holding out one hand and trying to retrieve the wayward foam rubber pads with the other. "I'm Nancy Kennedy, the world's only three-breasted hunchback."

Once we were both seated and I'd shifted to the right, she leaned forward. "You won't believe the lengths people go through to try and impress me. It's refreshing to see you're secure enough not to fall into that trap."

I just smiled and tugged at my skirt as it rode up my knees. We were halfway through our Caesar salads when I realized I hadn't even taken note of my companion's outfit. That's when I noticed she wore a simple turtleneck. I covered my mouth to conceal a smile. I peeked under the tablecloth. Another concealed smile: matching comfy-looking slacks. I looked again and this time couldn't hide my delight—sensible, open-toed shoes. Now that's what I call a "power outfit."

Dear Lord, I give You my wardrobe. Clothe me in the beauty of humility, for that will never go out of style. Help me to dress in the glory of Your gentleness, topped with the attitude of graciousness. May these garments impress all I meet so they will know I am well dressed because I am a daughter of the King. Amen.

Mid-Hen Crisis

Becky Freeman

*They will still bear fruit in old age,
they will stay fresh and green.*

Psalm 92:14

Sometimes I look at myself in the mirror and think, *Not bad for a thirty-nine-year-old chick.* Other times I look in the mirror and wonder, *Who let that ol' goose into the henhouse?* Being smack in the middle of midlife reminds me a lot of my middle-school years, when I was too old to be a cute little kid and too young to be a key-carrying, free-wheeling teenager. I lived in kid purgatory for a few years there. Now I'm in middle-aged no-man's-land: too old to be considered a young chick, too young to be a wise old hen.

You know who I envy these days? Surprisingly, it is not the Cindy Crawford types posing on covers of magazines. No, the women I envy look more like Barbara Bush. I'm looking forward to the old-hen stage—when my age will fall closer to the national speed limit. Here in the middle ages, it is becoming such an effort to keep up appearances. My makeup bag bulges with under-eye concealer, feather-proof lip liner, and a multitude of wrinkle erasers. My new skin lotion sounds like a name for a sorority house: Alpha Beta Hydroxy Complex (with microbeads no less. I don't know what they do, but they sure sound impressive, don't they?). I can't wait to be far enough away from youth that I can legitimately throw in the anti-aging towel and get on with growing good and old.

Who decided we had to try so hard to stay young anyhow? I love those happy clusters of silver-haired women you see exiting from tour buses—the kind whose very attire and demeanor says, "Who cares? I'm over seventy, and I'm entitled"; the sort who have memorized the poem, "When I Am Old I Shall Wear Purple" and embraced its philosophy and wardrobes. When an eighty-year-old woman wears orange stretch pants, a purple polyester shirt, Nike tennis shoes, and a hot-pink visor, folks call her "fun loving" and "young at heart." But we of the pushing-forty crowd would be labeled something altogether different if we donned the same ensemble. I say it's reverse age discrimination.

The over-seventy age group also gets lots of financial perks—like Medicaid and a cheap cup of coffee at

McDonald's. On the other end of the spectrum, the under-seven age group also fares well in the penny-pinching department: Little kids are always being given free stuff—balloons and candy and toys in their kiddy meals. But markdowns or freebies for "in-betweeners" are nonexistent. When was the last time you saw a sign that read "middle-age discount?"

I've been thinking about this disparity for a while, and as a result, I have a dream, a new vision for change. Remember that Million-Man March on America's capitol a few years back? Well I think we ought to organize a "Middle-Aged Women's Waddle on Washington" in a collective effort to make our society more mid-lifer friendly. I've even written a speech outlining the changes I'd like to see.

> If I, a woman of the middles ages, were in charge
> of the country—
> Donuts would be declared a health food.
> Walking into a room and forgetting why you are
> there would be a sign of genius.
> Men's pajamas, size extra large, would be
> considered elegant evening wear.
> Glasses and car keys would holler, "Right here!"
> when you ask aloud, "Where did I put them?"
> The word "plump" would be interchangeable
> with the words "sexy" and "attractive."

Everyone would agree to always be late to
everything. (This way, we'd all get there at
the same time. I don't know why someone
hasn't thought of this one already.)

And if I were in charge of the country—
Wrinkles on faces could be starched and ironed.
Twenty-year-olds could take your aerobics classes
for you.
Teenagers would always be asking, "What else can
I do to help you, Mother?"

If I were in charge of the country—
On long car trips, husbands would be required
to periodically ask their wives, "How would
you like to stop at that cute little gift shop,
have some tea and scones, and shop for an
hour or so?"
A sense of humor and a kindhearted nature
would be valued more highly than being
skinny or young or beautiful.

The End.

If we could somehow manage to get these few items
changed, the word "midlife" might not be paired so
often with the words "crisis" or "crazies" or "malaise."
Instead, we'd hear maturing women announce, "I'm in

midlife bliss." Or "I'm at that ol' midlife prime—I love my life, and I like who I am. God is good."

Come to think of it, I *am* in love with my life, I *do* like who I am, and God *is* good—even at thirty-nine and holding.

Maybe we ought to hold off on that Waddle to Washington for a while. For even though our midlife bodies are a little baggier here and there, these mid decades can be the most fulfilling of our lives. I recently heard a man say, "I think women have this incredible 'blossoming thing' happen when they turn forty. They get an extra boost of confidence or something, and it's like they suddenly say, 'Look out world! I'm coming out of my shell!'"

I think he may be right. But before I hatch out of my middle-aged shell and go take over the world, I have one last important question to ask: "Does anybody remember where I put my car keys?"

Dear Lord, I celebrate the life You have given me. No matter where I am on my journey, You are with me. Guide my steps so that I may someday, at my journey's end, return my gift to You. Amen.

Grief

Sorrow's garden is perfumed in hope.

Erica Wise

Parachute Answers

Linda Evans Shepherd

Do not fear, for I am with you; do not be dismayed, for I am your God. I will strengthen you and help you; I will uphold you with my righteous right hand.

Isaiah 41:10

I used to think God was sometimes far away from me when I needed Him most. But my three-year-old son helped me change that belief. When we drove near the Loveland airport, Jimmy would often spy the silhouette of a parachutist floating to the ground. I never knew what impression this had on him until the day we drove by the scattered wreckage of a car crash. Lights flashed and emergency personnel shuttled victims into waiting ambulances.

Seeing the crumpled vehicles caused my mind to flash back to the afternoon, several years before, when my own car had crashed. I remembered hunching over the body of my young daughter after she had been thrown into the freeway, still strapped in her car seat. I had knelt on the damp pavement, wondering if Laura would live or die as I screamed for help. The answering sirens shifted my thoughts to the present, and my voice jolted to prayer.

"Jesus," I called, as I slowed the speed of my van to a traffic-jam crawl. "Those people being loaded into the ambulances need Your help! Don't let them die. Show them how much You love them."

I was startled when Jimmy shouted a prayer of his own. "Jesus!" he called. "Help those people! Put on Your parachute and get down here!"

At first, I felt compelled to explain Jesus didn't wear a parachute.

But as I thought about it, the more tangible Jimmy's picture of Jesus seemed. As I looked skyward, I could almost picture Jesus and a multitude of angels gliding toward the rescue operation on the wings of heavenly silk.

Suddenly, the memory of my own tragedy changed. Instead of seeing myself alone on the side of the highway, crying over the limp body of my injured daughter, I pictured Jesus by my side. At the time of the accident, I was unaware of His presence. But as I replayed the scene in my mind, I could almost see His arm around my shoulders. I could imagine His compassionate face as I cried out to Him for help.

This new perspective of my own tragedy caused me to wonder if my son's idea of Jesus floating down from the heavens was in fact more real than my idea that Jesus had been removed from my hurt and pain. After all, King David said, *The LORD is near to those who have a broken heart* (Psalm 34:18 NKJV).

So, although Jesus hadn't really worn a parachute the day of our accident, He had really brought me comfort and healing. Over time, He turned my tragedy into triumph and my sorrow into joy.

Since the afternoon of Jimmy's parachute prayer, I look up when things look grim, expecting to see a heavenly parachute floating in my direction.

After all, while I waited ten months for my daughter, Laura, to awaken from her coma following our car crash, I was never alone. He was with me even when I did not recognize His presence.

Dear Lord, there are times I am tempted to think You have abandoned me. Yet those are the times You are the closest. When grief wraps me in pain, I cannot always feel Your presence. Please lift the shroud of my grief and let me know You are near. Amen.

Bouquet

Patsy Clairmont

Be imitators of God, therefore, as dearly loved children and live a life of love, just as Christ loved us and gave himself up for us as a fragrant offering and sacrifice to God.

Ephesians 5:1-2

*O*ne sunny, spring day, Les came bounding into our home embracing two apricot sweetheart rosebuds for me. I, of course, was delighted.

The flowers had come with a powdered mix to lengthen their blooming time; I stirred it into the water. I gave each rose a fresh cut and then slipped them into one of the many vases collected from Les's continued courting of me. I sat my mini-bouquet in the living room, being careful to protect it from direct sun and yet giving it visibility for my enjoyment.

As the days went by, I was fascinated by what happened. My seemingly identical roses responded very differently to their environment. One slowly began to open, and at each stage of development, she was exquisite. Her unfolding presentation pleased me and added beauty and wonder to the room. Finally, my apricot beauty dropped her petals in a breathtaking farewell performance.

In contrast, the other rose seemed stuck in her beginning. She held tenaciously to her baby form. In the end, the brooding bud turned brown and hung over the edge of the vase like a tragic teardrop.

For days I thought about the contrasting visual. I've always applauded rosebuds as being so romantic. Yet there was something sad and unnatural about seeing a flower begin and end at the same place. The bud that didn't open never reached her potential. She never released the sweet fragrance placed within her to share with others. Her death portrayed regret and sadness.

I could celebrate even the loss of the open rose, knowing she accomplished all she was designed to do. Her fragrance lingered in our home even after the vase was removed.

My friend Vella was a flower in the fullest sense. When she was told she had only a short time to live and that her cancer was the most painful of cancers, instead of closing up, she spread her petals all the way open and bathed us in the fragrance of faith. We would not have blamed her if she had drawn into a bud and died privately in her pain.

But Vella saw this illness as her farewell performance, an opportunity for as long as she had left to fulfill the design God had for her. Vella lived out her remaining days with exquisite grace. Dropping her last petal, her parting words were, "Praise the Lord." Then she fell asleep and was gone.

Family and friends could celebrate her life and her home-going. At the time of this writing, it has been eleven years since she left us . . . and her fragrance still lingers.

I want, whatever my environment, to be growing and fragrant. I don't want to be closed and unable emotionally to open up to others. I don't want to die holding to myself what I should have given away.

Les's gift of roses, pressed between the pages of my memory, has been a poignant reminder: Openness is a risk, growth is its reward, and His grace makes it all possible.

BOUQUET

Dear Lord, may my life be like a fragrant rose, blossoming and open to all You have for me. Give me Your grace to bloom where You have planted me, despite whatever circumstances I face. Help me to be open so that I may live life to its fullest. Amen.

When Gifts Have Wings

Susan Duke

*Every good and perfect gift is from above,
coming down from the Father of
the heavenly lights, who does not
change like shifting shadows.*

James 1:17

It's here! I shouted inwardly, as I pulled the loosely rolled package from my post office box. Since we live in the boonies, my husband usually retrieves the mail on his way home from work. But when I'm expecting something special, I make the five-mile drive into our small town myself.

And now at last, the package I was anticipating had finally arrived. My hands trembled as I carried it to my car and sat it on the seat beside me. I was tempted to rip it open and peek inside, but I didn't dare disturb the contents without proper respect for its unveiling. I had no choice but to take it home, where, in privacy, my unpredictable emotions could have free reign.

I'd never experienced a moment like this. It was a "first." It was a new dimension in my life, a new beginning. It was a rainbow-after-the-rain, happy-and-sad-at-the-same-time moment. And it would forever mark a page in the journal of my heart.

When I finally got back home, I felt I was moving in slow motion as I found a comfortable chair in which to sit and began to open the package. But I couldn't sit still. I had to stand. Carefully, I removed the tape that sealed the plastic covering and pulled out three complimentary copies of *Home Life* magazine. Inside was the first story I'd ever written, the first story I'd ever sent to a publisher, and the first time I would ever see that story and my name in print.

I thought with amazement of the thousands of people that would be reading something I had poured onto paper from my heart. I was holding a miracle in my hands.

I had good reason to feel especially sensitive about the copies of the December issue I received that cold, blustery, November day. The story was about an uncanny dream I had about a star on the first Christmas after losing our eighteen-year-old son, Thomas. I had told this story on speaking occasions when I was specifically asked to give my testimony. I often referred to it as "my star story." Many times people asked if I had it written down and said they would like to share it with others. I always said, "No, but one day I will write it."

Before sending in my manuscript, I had wrestled with the title. I wanted to call the story "A Gift from Thomas," but I kept telling myself the editors would probably prefer something simpler, so I decided to call it "The Star." I took a deep breath, turned the page, and there, across a layout of a beautiful night sky, were the words, "A Gift from Thomas." Tears of joy slid down my cheeks as I realized the editor had discarded my make-do title and given my tribute the very title I had envisioned. And that wasn't all. I couldn't help wondering, *Is it just a coincidence that this magazine has arrived today—November eighth—Thomas's birthday?*

Earlier that day, I had ordered a dozen balloons from a local gift shop. I decided that instead of taking flowers to the cemetery for Thomas's birthday, I would take colorful balloons, release them, and watch them until they were out of sight, sending a birthday message of love heavenward to Thomas.

What had already transpired that day was extraordinary enough, and I almost felt guilty asking for more. But, on my way to pick up the balloons, I found myself praying for one more little sign. "Lord, let me know somehow that Thomas has been part of this day."

As the clerk handed me the colorful mass of balloons, she hesitated. "Would you like another dozen balloons to go with those?" she asked. "I made a mistake on an order earlier. So if you want these, I'd like for you to have them." Then, before I could reply, she added, "And you know, I also have this giant Happy Birthday balloon. You are welcome to that one, too, if it's a birthday you're celebrating."

I thanked her and walked out of the store virtually covered with balloons. The significance of what had just happened didn't occur to me until I was well on my way to the cemetery. "How many balloons do you have?" whispered a still, small voice.

I did a quick count. I ordered a dozen and the clerk gave me another dozen, that was twenty-four and then the Happy Birthday balloon made twenty-five.

"And how old is Thomas today?" the voice prodded.

"Twenty-five," I whispered.

Once again, God had heard the cries of a mother's heart. A day filled with loss and disappointment became a day of rejoicing and celebration as I envisioned Thomas standing with the Creator of all birthdays, smiling and waiting for twenty-five balloons to make their journey across Heaven's gates.

I got out of the car at the cemetery, gathered the balloons from the back seat, and walked to the spot where I would set them free. One by one, I let them go. Compared to the vastness of Heaven, I felt small as I watched the kaleidoscope of colors dance upward into the blue sky. I waited to send the last and biggest balloon—the huge, silver, Happy Birthday balloon. I hugged it tight, kissed it, and released it to deliver my celebration of love to Thomas.

As the silver message faded from sight, I realized that there is no distance between Heaven and hearts. I'd touched Heaven and held its splendor in my hands. Celebrating life, both here and there, we exchanged gifts . . . gifts with wings.

Dear Lord, help me to remember there is no distance between my heart and You. You are aware of all my hopes and dreams. Lord, like a kaleidoscope of balloons, I release each one to Your care. For only through You will my hopes and dreams soar to heavenly heights. Amen.

Either Way

Kelly J. Martindale

*He heals the brokenhearted
and binds up their wounds.*

Psalm 147:3

"Hi, this is Linda," I heard the caller say to the machine one day. I immediately recognized that the cheerful caller had already left several messages. "I want to invite you to a writer's conference," she continued, repeating the same message she had left in the past. I felt a flood of guilt knowing I had not returned any of her calls.

"Hello Linda," I said picking up the phone. "I appreciate the invitation. I really would like to go, but it's not a good time. We lost our daughter a few months ago."

Linda expressed sincere sorrow for my loss, but unlike others, she didn't push. Somehow, she seemed to understand.

A few months later, another invitation arrived. With Linda's encouragement, I accepted and stepped cautiously from the refuge of my home. When I arrived at the conference, the first person I saw was Linda. She invited me out for a cup of coffee afterward, and I agreed.

We began with introductions and small talk, but we soon moved to the subject of writing. Linda handed me an article she had written. I was excited to read it. I admired her for following her dreams, for letting God guide her.

She remained silent as I read her article. Tears welled in my eyes as the words leapt from the page into my soul. Finally, I understood how, with so few spoken words, she had been able to comfort me.

Her story recounted the aftermath of the car accident in which her eighteen-month-old daughter, Laura, had been critically injured. Just three years earlier, she and her family had waited anxiously to see if little Laura would live or die as they earnestly petitioned God for her life.

Linda had experienced the anxious minutes that seemed like hours and the hours that disguised themselves as days. She knew the torment of praying, "Lord, not my will but Thine be done." She knew the desperation a mother feels when she can no longer protect her child.

Linda's prayers were answered—Laura lived. Her permanent injuries, however, have resulted in the establishment of a new "normal" in their home as they determine to dream new dreams. Our daughter did not live, and that result has also made it necessary to establish new "norms" for our family. Our dreams were shattered, but glory to God, we are beginning to dream again.

I look at Linda's life, and I look at mine. Both of us must depend upon God's grace to face the future with hope and find the bright spots in our days. Too many people let their lives be destroyed by tragedy. They give up, refusing the comfort and encouragement God provides.

I've learned some lessons from Linda—be persistent, yet gentle. I'm grateful she didn't quit calling me. I've learned also to let my heart guide my words, knowing that just a few spoken carefully can comfort deeply.

Dear Lord, I know that sorrow comes to all.
You never promised to take me around it,
above it, or below it, but to take me through it.
Thank You for being with me in my
sad times as well as my times of joy. Amen.

My Friend Betty

Nancy Hoag

Where, O death, is your victory?
Where, O death, is your sting?

1 Corinthians 15:55

*O*ne bitter and downcast spring day, I approached the door of a stranger and found not only a friend but a lifeline.

My case brimming with beauty products, I nudged the doorbell and shifted from one foot to the other as I watched a woman sprinting toward me. She was slightly plump and was wearing denims and a red-checked shirt. Her hair was short and windblown, and her eyes danced behind horn-rimmed glasses. A poodle stood beside her. As she smiled, I was amazed at her beauty.

Inside, as she surveyed my catalog, I watched her radiant face, listened to her voice, and inhaled the fragrance of pot roast drifting throughout the house.

She didn't seem to be in a hurry, so we talked. I sensed a warmth about her home that ours didn't possess. There was a decorative fish with "Jesus" on its belly, and the walls in the kitchen and entry were covered with religious pictures and prayers. Betty's open Bible was nearby but, unlike the Bible at our house, it was falling apart from constant use.

Betty's youngest, freckle-faced Christopher, darted into the room for hugs. Under his baseball cap, I caught sight of his mom's smile. Kids hopped and pushed through the house. Even the dog leaped in unrestrained anticipation. The house was happy, and Betty seemed to be the reason. *She's special,* I thought as she grinned.

Betty talked about her family and then asked about mine. I know she was shocked when I suddenly headed for the door, tears welling up in my eyes. But somehow, she was able to keep me talking for another hour as I unloaded my problems and frustrations.

"Will you come back?" she asked as I was finally leaving.

"Definitely not!" I exploded, collecting my wits and my samples. "I've already taken too much of your time," I apologized.

However, as I crammed catalogs into my bag, Betty's voice became firm. "All right. I'll have to come to your house, then," she said. My resistance conquered, I nodded an "okay," rushed to my car, and hurried to home and seclusion.

The following day, Betty made the first of many visits. She never seemed too busy for me, coming as often as I'd allow. I'd share, weep, complain, and question—and she'd listen, read from her Bible, and pray. Betty was unlike any Christian I'd ever known.

I felt certain I was a Christian myself. I'd accepted the Lord in high school. There'd been Sunday school and camp. I sang with the adults and directed the youth. I'd played the piano, joined the women's group, and taught Bible school. My babies were baptized and fell asleep nightly to "Jesus loves you; this I know." I did know Jesus loved them—but I didn't know He loved me, too. Until Betty.

When I had shared problems with my Christian friends in the past, they had tried to help by offering scriptures and books. "We'll pray at our next meeting," they had promised. They meant well, but no one had taken the time to really listen and understand what I was going through. My life seemed beyond hope, complete with a divorce that climaxed the years of thin commitment and unforgiveness. Finally, I had withdrawn.

When Betty visited, she did pray *for* me, but she also prayed *with* me. She suggested scriptures to read, but she also brought a bag of Bibles and devotionals, and we read together. She even dialed a Christian station on my radio and ordered, "Leave it there."

Betty suggested, pleaded, chided, and argued until I bought my own Bible—a translation I finally understood. Then she suggested I attend a Bible study. When I balked, she drove me to the church and signed us both up!

Eventually, Betty realized I needed a professional counselor, and she told me so. I said I'd see one. But she knew. On our way to lunch, she drove to a counseling center and introduced me to the staff. When I wasn't certain I could handle the fee, she offered to pay. Betty anticipated my every need, checked with the Lord, and often astounded me with the plans she made for us.

Near the end of my counseling, Betty said she had tickets for a luncheon—with Christian women, a "special" speaker, and prayer. "And," she said, "you are going."

Honestly! This is absolutely the last straw, I thought. *My counselor says I'm growing. Yes, there's something "small" bothering me, but I'm better!* However, I soon discovered God doesn't settle for "better." It's His best He wants for and from us.

Midway through lunch, the speaker began to talk about inner healing and being done with painful memories—and I took it all in. After weeks of prayer and preparation, I received complete release and walked away from my anger, filled with joy.

For a while, we continued our weekly study together—until I began teaching in a Christian school and Betty resumed her ministry to whomever God sent her way. Coveting stolen minutes together, we'd meet for lunch or coffee and talk about what the Lord was doing in our lives. Even when I traveled, I always knew she was there—at the other end of the line—ready to share and pray—until one year later when the Lord called her home.

Doctors had given Betty two years; God gave her five.

She might have become angry and bitter. She might have withdrawn, but she never did. Even when she was hindered by pain, she worshipped God, studied the Scriptures, and told others about Him—even from her hospital bed. Betty, in her quiet and unassuming way, never stopped ministering.

When she died, I felt angry at times. I didn't understand. But, because the Lord had become my life, my grief did not consume me. Betty was gone, but God had used her to reveal to me a great truth: *Living* His Word is the true manifestation of faith.

Someone has said, "If you give a man a fish, you feed him for a day. If you teach him to fish, you feed him for life."

Betty taught me to fish.

❧

Dear Lord, thank You for the people You have put into my life. Their love changes my world, and my heart overflows with love for them. May I make a difference in their lives as well. Amen.

Wisdom

The greatest use of life is to spend it for something that will outlast it.

William James

Polliwogs in the Straining Cloth

Gwendolyn Mitchell Diaz

*He that handleth a matter
wisely shall find good.*

Proverbs 16:20 KJV

Halima was a working woman. Hers was not just an ordinary forty-hour work week. Hers was backbreaking labor from dawn till dusk, seven days a week. The pressures of working, raising children, and trying to maintain some kind of home life were heavy, especially since she found herself living in a nomadic society that offered very few conveniences, and even fewer rights, for its women.

I was very young when I first met Halima. She was—well, I'm not really sure how old she was. Let's just say from the looks of her gnarled fingers and wrinkled brow, she was "well worn." She was from a Fulani tribe in West Africa that wandered its way through the deep "bush country" where my dad ran his leprosy clinics.

Each week I would watch for Halima. I could see her coming down the long path that led to our kitchen door. Her walk was tall and smooth—almost elegant. Her hips swayed rhythmically back and forth as her bare feet kicked up a dusty cloud along the sandy trail. Her head was ramrod straight, and a huge gourd filled with milk rode steadily on top.

As Halima approached, she became even more fascinating. The sun flashed off her bright red fingernails, dyed from many hours spent soaking in berry juices. As she drew near, I could distinguish the big, tin hoops in her ears, the dark patches on the faded blue cloth wrapped around her lower body, and her big toothless grin. I always smiled "real big" at Halima so that she would have to smile back. That way, I could see if she had any new gaps where she used to have teeth. I worried about how she would eat if she lost many more.

Once she arrived, Halima would sit on her haunches, chewing on bark with her few remaining teeth, while my mother measured the milk and sent it into the kitchen to be strained and boiled. I sat watching from my swing that hung low from the nearby mango tree. Halima would thank my mother for her generous payment (a few tin cans as well as a few round shillings), and she would head back down the lonely dirt path.

Over time, my mother began to suspect that something might be wrong with the milk. It seemed thinner than usual. Was Halima doctoring the milk, watering it down in order to get a few more shillings for her hard labor and her long walk?

"No! No!" Halima protested in her native tongue. "Halima would never do that. It must be the cows. They are weak. The sun is too strong. The grass is too sparse. There is only thin milk to sell. It is all the cows have to offer!"

But the evidence proved her wrong. One day, swimming in the middle of the straining cloth, were three tiny polliwogs. It turned out that for months, Halima had stopped at a pond on the way to our house. There she had filled her gourd to the top with tepid water. She had tried carefully to remove any evidence. But that day, little eggs had slipped in unnoticed and hatched while she journeyed down the long, winding path to our house.

That was the last time I remember seeing Halima and her big toothless grin. She had cheated. Then she had lied. She had been caught. Now she was gone.

I wondered who would buy her milk. Who would watch for her down the long winding paths of her life? Who would care about her teeth or count the patches on her skirt?

I soon forgot about Halima. There were plenty of other interesting characters who were more than happy to sell us milk. But I'll always remember the lesson she taught me. No matter what the pressures are or how easy or justifiable it seems, cheating is never worth it. Sooner or later you get caught because sooner or later there are bound to be polliwogs flip-flopping in someone's straining cloth.

Dear Lord, help me to remember that no advantage, small or large, is worth losing my integrity. Give me a nudge when I am tempted to compromise and let a little dishonesty sneak in. For keeping my heart clean is wise, and it will bear the fruit of goodness in my life. Amen.

Free Gift, Free Gift

Naomi Rhode

Whoever is thirsty, let him come; and
whoever wishes, let him take the
free gift of the water of life.

Revelation 22:17

She wore black to mourn her mother's death. A school teacher and part of the group to which I was speaking in Rostov-on-Don, Russia, she drew my heart to hers in a special way with her sad, wistful, intelligent persona.

We were in Russia at the request of the minister of education to teach a curriculum of Judeo-Christian ethics and values to school teachers and administrators. Speaking through my translator, Jane, I had referred several times to the free gifts given to us—free gifts that life gives us, free gifts that God gives us. Her skepticism

FREE GIFT, FREE GIFT

and resignation to the life and system in which she had been immersed was evident in her body language.

"I don't understand, free gift. I don't understand free gift . . . ," she repeated several times.

We had chosen to wear very basic-looking clothes and no jewelry on this privileged journey, respecting the basic lifestyle of the Russian people. The poverty experienced by so many was a stark contrast to the abundance of America. However, at the last minute while I was packing, I had decided to wear an inexpensive ring I had loved. As I slipped it on my finger, I prayed that God would show me to whom I was to give it.

At the end of our Thursday-afternoon session, Vera, my friend in black, stayed to talk further with me. Her questions were profound; her face portrayed the stress and trauma of her personal journey. Again, she said, "I don't understand . . . free gift!"

Give her the ring, I sensed the Lord urging me. But noticing her stocky fingers, I hesitated. *It won't fit,* I lamented. Then I said good-bye to Vera, walked through the long hall, down the stairs, and out of the Palace, past Lenin's statue to our waiting bus. As I boarded the bus, I sensed the Lord urging me again. *Give her the ring!*

Okay, Lord, I promised.

I ran back up the stairs, through the long hall, and into the ballroom. Vera and the translator were sitting alone in the room. As I quickly pulled the ring from my finger, I watched the tears of disbelief fill her eyes. Placing the ring on her little finger, I smiled, hugged her, and said, "free gift."

Friday was our last day with our wonderful new friends. They came with arms full of peonies, lilacs, and roses. They sang and danced for us in gratefulness for friendship, sharing, and the curriculum we had presented. Vera was the last to leave the room, and she shyly approached me with a beautiful four-color book on art throughout the ages. It was written in English. Based upon the salary of schoolteachers and the prices in Russia, the book probably represented a major portion of a month's earnings. With love, pride, and in English, with tears in her eyes, she said, "Now I understand free gift, free gift."

Dear Lord, I thank You for the generous free gifts You have bestowed on me. Just as You have reached out to me and given of Your very best, teach me to reach out to others. Amen.

The Flower Garden

Mary van Balen Holt

Sow your seed in the morning, and
at evening let not your hands be idle,
for you do not know which will succeed,
whether this or that, or whether
both will do equally well.

Ecclesiastes 11:6

*O*utside our kitchen door is a small garden space.
Early in the spring, I loosened the soil and planted the
flowers. The snapdragons, asters, and pinks were
seedlings. The rest were started from seed—bachelor
buttons, a few marigolds, dependable zinnias. They fill
in the empty space around the perennial lavender,
columbine, and flax. I like flowers that grow tall, look a
bit unkempt, and make lovely bouquets in the summer.
So, I planned and planted.

One corner bloomed first. A small cluster of blue flax and some yellow coreopsis were the perfect backdrop for bright red carnations. At the opposite end of the garden, an old lavender plant began shooting up the fragrant foliage with its promise of a bloom in its tightly closed buds.

After its first burst of color, the garden limped through summer. The asters, labeled, "tall, perfect for cutting," turned out to be dwarf plants. Few flowered. The snapdragons did not bush out as they usually do, and only a few bachelor buttons germinated. A wild columbine, given by a friend, bloomed and threatened to take over, and the zinnias, my least favorite, yielded the most blooms. The garden looked spotty at best. I looked in vain for the flowers I had planted. Disappointed, I picked a bouquet of zinnias with a token snapdragon or two and placed them around the house.

One afternoon, while staring at the patch from the steps outside the kitchen, I realized that if I would forget the garden I carried around in my head, the one I had wasn't so bad.

The zinnias added lots of color. The lavender had spread and was in full bloom. Even if few, the red and yellow snapdragons were tall. If trimmed, the coreopsis

~

would bloom all summer. I just had to learn to love the garden that grew, not the one I had planted!

Dear Lord, help me remember that my ways are not always Your ways. Life does not always unfold as I plan or imagine. Help me accept the imperfections, the changes, and the unexpected events that come into my life. Teach me to embrace what I am given, without wasting my time grieving for what might have been. Amen.

A Child's Wisdom

Cheryl Kirking

A little child will lead them.

Isaiah 11:6

A few years ago, we decided to give my father a surprise birthday party. My son, who was then four, was especially excited about the party for his grandpa. Bryce spent all day making streamers and paper hats and decorating the house. He instructed his brother and sister where they should hide and how to yell "Surprise!" with the proper inflection and zeal.

When the moment of Grandpa's long-awaited appearance finally arrived, Bryce led the troops in the noisy revelry. But, as so often happens in life, reality failed to meet expectations. The party horns refused to toot properly, the guests weren't appropriately enthusiastic, and the cake wasn't chocolate. Finally, Bryce could take no more disappointment and melted into a sobbing little heap on the floor. Scooping him up in my arms, I took him to a quiet room where he poured out his troubles to me.

"Sweetheart," I asked, as he flopped across on my lap, "what can we do to help you feel better?"

"Oh, Mommy," he cried between heaving sobs, "can we rewind the party?"

"Honey, I wish sometimes that we could do that, but we can't rewind time," I answered, smoothing his golden hair from his damp forehead. "But we can start from right now and find a way to make the rest of the day better."

"Well," he sniffed, "maybe—maybe we could just hit 'pause' a little while before we go back, okay."

"That's a good idea," I answered.

As I quietly rocked my little boy, smelling his sweet hair and feeling his warm little body relax, I realized what an important lesson I had just learned from my child. Sometimes, when life is overwhelming, the best thing to do is to just "hit pause" for a little while.

Dear Lord, how I would like to rewind parts of my life. Sometimes I feel so overwhelmed by it all. Please teach me how to rest in You so I can have a fresh outlook on the situations of my life. Amen.

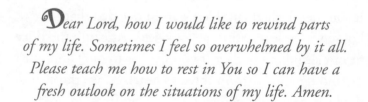

Cottage Contentment

Mary Kay Shelby

*I have learned to be content
whatever the circumstances.*

Philippians 4:11

"**D**UPLEX. 2 BEDROOM, FENCED YARD, SAILBOAT BEND AREA, $450/MONTH, CALL 555-1125."

I was intrigued but not hopeful. I knew that a house in south Florida couldn't be much to look at with the rent so low, but I was interested in the "Sailboat Bend" part. It sounded Bohemian. Derek and I decided that the house was at least worth a "look-see." After all, the price fit our shrinking budget (two incomes to one) and our expanding family (from three to four). So we traveled to the little neighborhood along the New River in Fort Lauderdale, in a cul-de-sac away from the main street.

I was right about the house. It was quite small, not more than six hundred square feet from bumper to bumper, and the carpet was hideous, a rusty-mud brown sculpture that had seen too much foot traffic. The path from the front door to the kitchen was completely matted down, the fibers no longer able to stand up by themselves. In another area, there was only a hint of the former creamy flooring now yellowed with bits of dirt permanently stamped into the crevices. There was no place for a washer and dryer—a necessity for a family of nearly four. "Ugh," I groaned. It had paneling—bona fide 1970s.

We took it anyway. *At least it doesn't have green shag carpet,* I reasoned. *That would be the one thing I couldn't take!*

We called it "the cottage." The day we moved in, I was struggling with its smallness. I couldn't imagine where we would stuff all of our belongings or how I would fit the baby's crib and Austin's bed into the same room, much less their clothes or toys. But as I looked around, I began to notice the unique personality this house had. The ceilings had whitewashed timber beams, and every room had abundant windows, which brought streams of sunlight that cast a glow in every paneled corner. I noticed a gentle breeze.

There was a lovely, spacious patio with an overhang where we put our picnic table. The yard was narrow, but fenced in so Austin could play outdoors to his heart's content. A fragrant lemon tree and an orange tree with juicy fruit shaded our lawn. Best of all, we had a beautiful view of the New River. A drawbridge was nearby, so every hour we heard the clanging of the bells, and we'd rush out to see what kind of boat was going by or who would wave back.

We fell in love with our cottage, and our time there was filled with laughter and joy.

A boardwalk followed the other side of the river, lined with palm trees and telescopes, a rain gauge, a barometer, and a huge sundial surrounded by inviting grass. Nearly every Sunday afternoon, we loaded the children in the stroller, filled the backpack with sandwiches, put our dog, Sam, on a leash, and trekked across the bridge to relax, run, and rejuvenate ourselves for the upcoming week. The hours spent lollygagging along the river were countless. It was there that Austin learned about fishing and boats. In our yard, the harvest of lemons gave us all the homemade lemonade we could ever want.

As precious as our cottage was, however, I still struggled. I constantly strategized "new and improved" ways to stuff blankets under beds and Tupperware in the oven. (The trick was remembering to take the Tupperware out of the oven before I turned it on.) The carpet only grew more flat and embedded with dirt when a certain two-year-old enthusiastically dragged in his mud-pie creations.

Somehow this didn't mesh so well with my desire to have people over and actually turn the lights on. So, we invited ourselves to other people's nice houses instead. While traveling to Atlanta, we got to visit friends who had recently moved into their brand new "even-picked-the-colors" home. The emerald carpet was so thick that I couldn't even see my feet. It took every ounce of willpower I had not to cry on the spot. Instead, I bit my lip and forced a smile as I was shown the second, third, and fourth bedrooms, all with closets as big as my bedroom.

I "oohed and ahhhed" at the loft, but finally had to excuse myself. I thought a restroom break would give me a chance to regain my composure. That's when I saw the sauna. Of course, nearly anyone would be a little green with envy after seeing this house, but I was already experiencing episodes when I visited in seemingly regular houses. How wonderful to be able to send the kids off to the playroom while the adults talked. I was becoming terribly frustrated. Driving home, I would often melt into tears. And then I would feel a burden of guilt for caring so much about material things.

Gently and persistently, God would somehow get my attention each time and remind me of His love and the wonderful little cottage He had provided for us. His tender reminders always put things into perspective. Sure, cream Berber carpet would be beautiful, but I wouldn't be able to let Austin run in and out of the house barefoot. A bigger house would mean more time spent cleaning and more money spent decorating. Ultimately, more time would be spent fussing, and less time would be spent rolling around on the floor with the children and then picking Play-Doh bits out of my hair. In essence, my kids' memories might revolve around my dancing with a vacuum rather than dancing with them. Which did I want more?

One of my cherished realizations was that we could have just as many intimate get-togethers at the cottage as we could in a palace, perhaps even more, for there was certainly less by which to be distracted. So we did just that; we invited people over for potlucks and pizza, movies, cards, and even a New Year's Eve party (cramming fourteen people into the house was a real feat!). Conversations lasted for hours on end, and the ties that bound us to those friends were strengthened. The joy of contentment deepened its roots in my heart.

We've since moved to Oregon, all of 3,741 miles from our home in Florida. Due to distance, we had to rent a house sight unseen. Talk about a step of faith! I took a deep breath and told God that whatever He provided would be fine with me. And I must admit, I was relieved when we pulled up in our moving truck. It is twice the size of the last, with a huge yard and a washer and dryer. It's cute.

But I've been thinking that God must not believe I've learned contentment fully yet, because the carpet—it's green shag.

Dear Lord, how I long for contentment. Help me to be thankful not only for what I have received, but for what I have escaped. Teach me to think of yesterday without regret and tomorrow without fear as I learn to have an attitude of gratitude. Amen.

Overcoming

*Contentment isn't getting
what we want but being
satisfied with what we have.*

Anonymous

Mother's Last Date

Jess Moody

Precious in the sight of the
LORD is the death of his saints.

Psalm 116:15

"Burt Reynolds dates my mother!"

Sounds like something from the tabloid by the checkout counter at Ralph's Grocery, but that's exactly what happened in 1967!

We had been told that our mother, Connie, was dying of cancer of the brain. It was irreversible and inoperable. She had come to West Palm Beach on what she knew was her last trip. She wanted to see those grandchildren—Pat and Martha—and her son and daughter-in-love (as she called Doris) just one more time.

MOTHER'S LAST DATE

〜

It was her "I'm-just-dropping-by-on-my-way-to-Heaven trip." That was exactly how she had worded it.

Outwardly, Mother seemed as strong as garlic; inwardly, she was three weeks from her eternal journey. This outward mother fooled us, lulled us with her wit and down-home humor into underestimating the gravity of her illness. In just three weeks, after her return home, Doris, Patrick, Martha, and I came into her room and found her sitting on her bed, uttering strange, unfamiliar words. We knew it meant that the cancer had reached a strategic part of her brain.

"What a nice young family! Have we met? Nurse, please introduce them to me!"

We all felt like a knife had pierced our hearts.

My mind raced back to her visit a few weeks earlier. During the night I had slipped into my bathrobe and walked quietly downstairs to her room, only to find that she wasn't there! We had been warned that the cancer in her brain could cause her to do strange things.

I searched the house—no Mother.

Where could she be at 4:00 A.M.?

When I went out onto the porch, there she was, sitting in a rocking chair, wrapped up in a blanket, facing the intercoastal canal that ran in front of our house. There was a bit of a chill in the predawn night. The moon was pouring liquid silver onto the water, cutting a light path across the intercoastal waters directly to where Mother was sitting. It was as if God were smiling on her lovely, but tired, face.

Her voice was not strong. The cancer had done its deadly work on her vocal chords. She squeaked her words out in kind of a breathy wheeze.

"I was—was just sitting here, loving God with my pain," she confided. "That is the one thing that most crowds my mind. It is, for now, my greatest possession."

She looked up, toward the moon—and past it.

"That's it, God. I give You my pain," she wheezed.

That was almost the last private conversation I had with my mother. The next day was crowded with things we all thought we had to do.

Mother sort of sat around, getting miffed if we stopped work to worry about her. She kept on painfully puttering around the house, trying to help as much as she could. About six that evening, she announced that it would probably be best if she went back to Texas— "maybe tomorrow." Death's cool breath was beginning to blow on the back of her neck. She knew she had to get back—and fast.

And then it happened—the date!

About seven that evening, our doorbell rang. It was Burt. There he stood, one gorgeous hunk. He held a one-rose corsage in his hand and motioned toward a brown Rolls convertible parked in front of the house.

"I have come to ask Connie out on a date," he said politely.

I was incredulous. "You mean—you mean my mother?"

"How many Connies are here?" he asked.

I was stunned. Here was America's number-one heartthrob, great beefcake superior, asking for a date with my mother.

Burt pinned the corsage to my bewildered mother's dress. Doris quickly appeared and wrapped her fur coat around Mother's shoulders.

"Did you have something to do with this?" I whispered to Doris as Mother was swept into the Corniche, down the lakefront, and into the night—by Burt Reynolds!

"That's for me to know and you to find out," she giggled.

"Do you think we can trust Burt with her?" Doris winked.

"I don't know. You know how she is," I kidded back.

Two hours later, Burt brought Mother home. He walked her to the front door, held her in his arms, and kissed her—right on the mouth!

After he was gone, Mother's eyes were shining.

"I just realized something," she said smiling. "I may be gone in a few days, but right now, I'm certain that I'm not dead yet!"

Two days later, a columnist wrote that Burt Reynolds was seen in the Petite Marmite Restaurant in Palm Beach, having an animated conversation—with his mother!

Connie would have loved that.

Dear Lord, thank you for the precious lives of Your saints. When they are no longer with us, we mourn because we miss them, yet we rejoice because they now live free from pain. Amen.

Blue Hen Party

Becky Freeman

Whenever the rainbow appears in the clouds,
I will see it and remember the everlasting
covenant between God and all living
creatures of every kind on the earth.

Genesis 9:16

It was near Thanksgiving, but I was feeling far from thankful. We'd just had our second baby in two years, and Scott had started a new construction business. The bad thing about the construction business is that it's so dependent on the weather, and the bad thing about the weather is it is so undependable. Weeks of rain had taken their toll on our family mood and budget.

One afternoon I put the boys down for a nap, never an easy trick for me. Catching two wide-awake little boys felt a lot like trying to herd baby chicks. After changing their diapers, nursing Zeke, and reading *Pat the Bunny* six times, I was often so exhausted I'd collapse onto the bed just to recover from the ordeal of their nap time.

But this afternoon I'd managed to stay awake—and aware. Aware that we had no money. Our checking account was dwindling fast, and every dollar had to be counted and stretched. No matter what anyone says about the dignity and challenges of being poor, believe me, it's no fun. Worrisome thoughts tumbled through my mind, one on top of the other. *How will we buy groceries? What about Christmas presents? Will we be able to pay our bills? Will we ever be able to afford a night out again?*

I was in the middle of a full-blown pity party. And then, I hatched a novel idea. Surely I wasn't the only person feeling like a boneless chicken in this season of plump, festive turkey dinners. I could expand this bleak experience of mine to include other out-of-work friends. I could invite people to come to my pity party!

Parties always got my motor going. I went to the kitchen and took out a big, brown grocery sack, sat down at the dining-room table, then tore it into 5-by-5-inch squares. On each square I wrote:

"You are invited to a Hard Luck Party. Come as you are. Nothing is too ragged for this social event. Bring a package of whatever cheap luncheon meat you can afford, and we'll make a five-foot-long Poor-Boy sandwich. Be prepared to share a hard luck story with the rest of us, and do your best to make it as pitiful sounding as possible; we all need cheering up."

Then I wrote the time, date, and location and put a stamp on the back of each homemade "brown sack" invitation.

It's been twenty years since that party, and to this day my friends still talk about how much fun it was. Instead of cleaning up for the occasion, I actually stirred up the disorder in my already cluttered house. The pictures hung askew on the walls, kids' toys lay scattered everywhere, the curtains were draped and looped in mass disarray. The men arrived dressed in ragged T-shirts or overalls, the women in old, faded cotton dresses that hung loose and limp. The children were adorned in pillowcases and paper bags—whatever old thing their parents found lying around.

When it came time to share our "hard luck" stories, the room exploded in laughter. Each couple exaggerated the dire urgency of its circumstance to ridiculous proportions of pitiful. At one point, one of the men reached for an old guitar and, with a sad southern accent, began to sing an impromptu ballad of despondency. "Poor and tired and pitiful ol' me, I'm drowning in a sea of misery. . . ."

We carried on like a bunch of whinin' hound dogs, singing one sad song after another until we felt great. Of all the parties I've ever given, this one beat them all. Not because it was creative or well planned or special, but because we so desperately needed to laugh, to empathize, to not feel alone in our situations. The comfort of a common bond is one of God's greatest ways to strengthen discouraged hearts.

I have a friend and neighbor, Ethel Sexton, who is what we country folk call "an absolute hoot." One day I heard what sounded like a bunch of chickens squawking and carrying on outside my front door. I looked at my daughter and said, "What's that?"

She peeked out the window and said, "Mom, it's Ethel. She's talking to Daddy in the driveway."

Ethel doesn't just talk, she enthusiates. Though Ethel came from a childhood where money was scarce as hens' teeth, she will tell you in a heartbeat that her childhood was rich. Ethel takes her message of joy all over the country, and every day she delivers a two-minute radio spot for KCBI here in the Dallas-Fort Worth area. She ends every show with a classic sign-off: "This is Ethel Sexton, reminding you to make your O-O-O-OWN SUNSHINE!"

In other words, when life gives you a bad turn, turn it into a party. When it rains, make your own "indoor sunshine." Not long ago I had a chance to put Ethel's motto to the test. It was the first year I'd actually made a profit from my writing. So I splurged, reserving a beach house for a sun-splashed week in Gulf Shores, Alabama. How our family anticipated those long, lazy days of nothing but sunshine. None of us were emotionally prepared for seven long, lazy days of nonstop rain.

In my whole life, I do not remember it raining for seven days straight—not anywhere, any time, or for any reason. Why did this have to happen during our one precious week of vacation? Each day I would walk out on the "sun deck" to watch a new storm gathering. "Oh, Lord," I'd whine with the fervency of a child begging for candy, "please, just a bit of blue, just a shimmer of sun. Please, God, please." Then with a clap of thunder, I'd get my unwanted answer. "Not today, child, not today."

When it finally occurred to me that the rain might never stop, that we might actually have to go home in an ark, I began to look in other directions for sunshine. One afternoon, I headed to the grocery store, purchased party supplies, a big fluffy cake sprinkled with confetti-like candy, candles, some cheap toy favors, and the best part of all—a bouquet of sunny yellow balloons.

When I drove up the driveway to the beach house, Scott met me as he was coming down the stairs.

"What have you done?" he asked, eyeing the bobbing balloons.

"We're going to have a party. I'm making my O-O-O-OWN SUNSHINE!"

Scott laughed and said, "I was just coming to tell you, I ran down the beach a little while ago and brought you the sun."

"See!" he said, pointing skyward like a boy showing off the puppy that followed him home.

Sure enough, between two clouds, a sliver of sunshine peeked through, pouring out light that shimmered like liquid diamond dust. Then Scott gestured toward the sky above the ocean, and the sight was so magnificent I felt tears sting my eyes. Using the mist of the rain, and that bit of sun, God had created a full rainbow for our viewing pleasure.

And it dawned on me then that God does not waste the rain in our lives. For without the rain, ultimately, our lives would be colorless. We'd be less appreciative, less compassionate people. We survive the rainy days by trusting the Son to shine from the inside out—by making our own sunshine in life's darkest corners. And finally, because there has been rain, the sun can paint a glorious rainbow.

The same is true in our hearts.

Whenever the rainbow appears in the clouds, I will see it and remember the everlasting covenant.

Dear Lord, You are invited to my pity party. To You I complain both day and night. But as I complain, remind me to see that Your love continues to shine through my problems in a way that splashes rainbows through my life. Thank You for making rainbows whenever I feel misty, for the glow of the rainbow comes from the light of Your love. Amen.

I'm Thankful for What We Still Have

Sandra Picklesimer Aldrich

*He will call upon me, and I will answer
him; I will be with him in trouble,
I will deliver him and honor him.*

Psalm 91:15

My husband, Don, had always been in charge of the car maintenance, so after his death, I was too exhausted to think about our station wagon's balding tires. But one afternoon, a blowout on the expressway forced me to enter the unfamiliar world of four-ply radials and speed ratings. I nodded at appropriate times as the salesman explained the importance of computerized spin balancing, but the strain showed.

The young man sensed my confusion. "Why don't you grab a cup of coffee next door while we get you all fixed up?" he suggested.

I nodded, and, with misty eyes, trudged outside. "Lord, I hate it that Don isn't here," I muttered. "He should be buying these tires. He should be making the financial decisions. He should be helping me raise Jay and Holly. I need some encouragement, Lord."

I wiped my eyes and turned toward the restaurant parking lot, where a young woman was standing next to her car's open hood. I offered to help, but she insisted the engine would start again in another fifteen minutes—after it cooled off. So we pushed it out of the way, and I invited her to have coffee with me.

"Are you married?" she asked as we held our steaming cups. When I told her Don had died the previous Christmas, I expected her to mutter, "Oh, I'm sorry."

Instead she shrugged. "How long were you married?"

"Sixteen and a half years," I stammered.

She took a sip of her coffee. "Did you love him?"

"Yes, very much."

"Did he love you?"

I smiled. "Oh, yes."

Again she shrugged. "Then you've already experienced more love than most of us ever have. Think of that instead of what you've lost."

Then she told about her divorce—the beatings, the custody battles, the continuing threats. Suddenly she looked at her watch. "Hey, I gotta get to work. But thanks for listening. It helped a lot."

She was gone before I could tell her how she had helped me. I stared at her empty chair, shaking my head at the bizarre way God had answered my tearful prayer. *Okay, Lord,* I thought. *I'll try to concentrate on what I have left instead of what I've lost. But You'll have to help me.*

A few weeks later, our first Thanksgiving without Don tested that determination. My husband's favorite holiday meal had always been the traditional turkey dinner. He'd invite the relatives, and I'd cook a twenty-two-pound bird with all the fixings.

This time, I couldn't bring myself to cook without him there. Kind friends invited us to share their dinner, but it seemed too soon for us to sit around the table with another family. We needed something different, something that would remind us of our blessings without stirring up painful realities of what we had lost. So I called the Salvation Army and offered the three of us as meal servers.

We spent the afternoon heaping food on sturdy paper plates—instead of my blue-and-white china—for single mothers, street people, the elderly, and even entire families who had fallen on hard times. *What had they lost?* I wondered. *What about the fifty-ish woman in the summer dress? Had her husband once whispered, "Great meal, hon,"* as he squeezed her shoulders? Or had he left her for someone younger?* At least I didn't have to deal with rejection, too. *What about the man in the shiny suit? Did he live alone in a hotel room? Did he come here for the company as well as the food?* I smiled at Jay and Holly. We still had each other.

When it was time to wipe the tables that afternoon, I whispered my thanks to the Lord for getting us through our first Thanksgiving as a family of three. Oh, I figured challenges would still sneak up on me, but at least I had a new weapon with which to face them—I could concentrate on what I still had instead of what I had lost.

Dear Lord, show me how to make the best of the situations that come into my life. Remind me to enjoy what I have and help me to stop worrying about what is beyond my reach. I give my situations to You. Help me see how blessed I am. Amen.

The Almighty Cure

Vickie Baker

When anxiety was great within me,
your consolation brought joy to my soul.

Psalm 94:19

"What do I think about a cure?" I repeated into the receiver. "Cure for what?"

My speaker phone rattled a reply. "Spinal cord injury."

I responded, "Well, to be honest, it doesn't rate very high on my priority list."

After I hung up, the question transported me back to another place and time. It was 1979, and I had run away and joined the circus, literally. I was part of a trapeze act and loved it. Every morning I would mumble to myself, "People aren't supposed to be this happy when they grow up, are they?"

Five years later, a split-second mistake in timing dislocated my spinal cord, crumbled my marriage, and shattered my career. (There are few openings for a quadriplegic trapeze artist.) After my injury, I naively believed all of society's boldface lies about my inferior gimp status.

This world, it seemed, did belong to the young, the beautiful, the able-bodied. Crips need not apply.

I spent nearly every waking moment reading about cell regeneration and looked to the "Almighty Cure" as my only hope. Why not? After all, I couldn't perform anymore, and I had no desire to do anything else. Life had backed me into a corner.

And I'd pretty well proved during those first few years that there was no way out. I had learned firsthand that a plastic vacuum cleaner hose melts when taped to an exhaust pipe. I never knew. With all the stupid TV I'd watched, why hadn't I heard of this? And how could I have known that starving myself to death would take so long? I figured on three, four weeks tops, not two months. I would have gotten it right, that last time, if a friend hadn't called the police. I couldn't even kill myself right.

Logically, it made sense to me to end my life. I figured that I'd always need a wheelchair, I'd always suffer from dizzyingly low blood pressure, I'd always be plagued by pneumonia, I'd always need attendant care—and nothing would ever change.

Late one night in my tiny hospital room, with no place left to run and nothing left to lose, I finally cried out to God for help. That night, for the first time since my arrival on the psych floor, I fell into a deep, restful sleep.

The next day, the oh-my-God-what-am-I-gonna-do feeling in my throat was gone. A new ringmaster had quietly slipped into my heart and now ran the show. Six weeks later I left with plans to return to school.

So now I have an altered definition of the "Almighty Cure." I no longer pin my happiness on the hope that I will rise out of my chair and walk, that I will regain the use of my hands, that I will troop with the circus once more. I find that the Old Testament prophet Nehemiah spoke the truth when he said, "The joy of the LORD is your strength." Joy, to me, is a deep-seated confidence that God is in charge of every area of my life. I don't have to go through it alone anymore.

Faith did not change my circumstances, but it changed me. I still use a wheelchair, suffer with hypo-tension, endure respiratory problems, and require attendant care. But on the inside, I have peace of mind.

These days, a hand brace, a computer, and a newfound passion for writing have allowed me to complete my first book. I can now reach out to others with words of encouragement—something every bit as exciting as when I reached out to children with a comedy trapeze act. The pay might not be so great, but the benefits are out of this world!

If the "Almighty Cure" came along tomorrow, would I sign up for it? I honestly don't know. Without my disability, I would be different, and I have no desire to be different. And, in most ways, I've already been cured.

Dear Lord, Your ways are not always my ways.
When life trips me, I get angry with You.
But thank You that I can give You even
my brokenness, and You will raise me up for
an even higher purpose. Your love gives me
hope and courage to face tomorrow.

A Sweet Fragrance

Debbie Brockett

*We are to God the aroma of Christ
among those who are being saved
and those who are perishing.*

2 Corinthians 2:15

The gleeful shouts of children floated on the crisp fall air as my feet crunched through a carpet of sienna leaves. Trying to ignore the voices, I headed for the park's nearby rose garden, hoping for some privacy among its prickly shrubs.

Plucking some petals from a yellow rose, I sniffed its sweet perfume before shoving my hands into my coat pockets. I thought about the chaos I'd left at home. Blending a family was tough, but today, it seemed impossible. Why couldn't my loved ones just work together?

Eventually I began to pray. "I'm worried about the future and confused about the gray areas of my life.

Please give me Your peace." I waited, expecting God to encourage me. A stiff breeze whipped my hair into my eyes as I stood, waiting, disappointed by His silence.

Angrily, I flicked at my hair, then noticed a sweet fragrance. Looking down at my hand, I saw the rose petals. In my frustration, I had crushed them. Their delicate veins showed through the discoloration, yet amazingly, they were still in one piece, and their fragrance was stronger than when I had first picked them!

God had answered me. Could it be that the crushing, bruising times of my life produced a stronger, sweeter spirit? With a new sense of hope, I headed home.

Dear Lord, thank You for hope. Hope holds my hand in the darkest of nights. It helps me see the tiniest flicker of light to show me where to place my next step. It guides me back to You. Amen.

On Missing Margo

Ginger Green as told
to Sherri Langton

*Praise be to the God and Father of our Lord
Jesus Christ, the Father of compassion and
the God of all comfort, who comforts us in
all our troubles, so that we can comfort
those in any trouble with the comfort we
ourselves have received from God.*

2 Corinthians 1:3-4

A sunny redhead. An honor student. Not the type of
girl you'd expect to see lying still and pale in a coroner's
room. But on Monday, May 13, 1991, there she was,
our daughter, Margo, dead at twenty-two. Murdered.

A few hours earlier, Margo's estranged husband, Eric,
had followed her to work, broad-sided her car with his,
and in full view of downtown commuters, shot her
seven times with a 9-millimeter automatic shotgun. Eric

then knelt beside her, pointed the gun to his temple, and ended his own life.

While these cold details numbed me, they couldn't soften what I saw through the glass separating me from the coroner's room. The instant I saw Margo, a spasm of horror stabbed me, and I dissolved into sobs. Every fiber in me wanted to smash through the glass, take Margo in my arms and cradle her.

"Jesus," I whispered, "hold her for me."

I'd seen Margo just the day before Mother's Day. She'd given me a card with a handwritten message: "Thanks for everything, especially your endless love and giving." Margo had modeled a new dress for her upcoming college graduation.

Had she lived, Margo would have graduated the following Saturday and filed for divorce from Eric, with whom she'd had an abusive four-year marriage, on Monday. I left Margo on Mother's Day with a hug and hope for her new beginning.

That Thursday at the funeral, God gave me the strength to stay composed before the open casket that held our daughter dressed in her graduation dress. Had it not been for the prayers and support of friends and extended family, I couldn't have endured it.

For days after the funeral, I clutched my last Mother's Day card from Margo and wept. I thanked God that in the last few weeks of her life, Margo had committed her heart and hurts to God. But while I knew she was in Heaven, I was still in the world, aching with my loss.

As I mentally relived Margo's teen years, I remembered when she first met Eric, the boy up the street. Margo had been fourteen at the time and Eric, twenty-one. He had spent every spare moment at our house. Margo was flattered that an older guy paid so much attention to her. Because Margo was so young, my husband, Chuck, and I set limits—no dating until age sixteen; curfews when dating begins; no boyfriends during our Sunday afternoon family time. We really never thought that when Margo started dating Eric at age sixteen, he would be the only one she dated.

We noticed that Eric seemed to want Margo to himself. He spent so much time with her that she hardly saw her friends and family. When Eric was at our house, he spoke to Margo but avoided Chuck and me. While his behavior disturbed us, we never suspected anything dangerous would come of it.

Over time, we began to see a change in Margo. She began challenging the rules we imposed on her dating as if she questioned our motives. "Eric says I should be able to stay out later," she informed us. Margo had always been an obedient daughter. Now it seemed Eric was turning her against us.

My uneasiness about Eric mushroomed into distrust on one particular occasion. Though it was rare, Margo went out one evening with Chuck and me and her older brother, Chase. Eric followed us in his car, and because Margo had told him we'd planned to stay out past her date curfew, he became infuriated and tried to run us off the road.

As Chuck tried to control the car, I tried to control my fears. *What kind of person is my daughter involved with?* I wondered. I was terrified, but Margo showed no fear. She tearfully pleaded with us to let her out of the car so she could calm Eric down.

Chuck and I never gave her the chance. That night when we got home, we laid down the strictest rule we'd ever given Margo: She and Eric couldn't see each other for six weeks, and Margo couldn't ride in a car with him for one year. We hoped that during this period Margo would find someone else.

But after their six-week separation, Margo drove herself to see Eric, and in about a year, they became engaged. Then Margo announced that she planned to move in with Eric on her eighteenth birthday.

Because of his behavior, I wasn't surprised that Eric was committed to this plan, but I felt sick about Margo.

We had tried to instill in her a love for God, but now it appeared that our daughter was choosing a relationship with Eric, with whom we still had serious reservations, over a relationship with God.

Chuck and I agonized, *Should we try to force an end to their relationship? What will happen if Margo marries and the marriage goes bad?* We wondered if we were being too hard on them, and we desperately hoped the marriage would succeed.

Reluctantly and prayerfully, we released Margo to her plans but refused to pay for the wedding. We warned her that if she married before finishing high school and at least one year of college, we wouldn't financially support her education. But despite these strategies, Margo married Eric shortly after she turned eighteen.

Within two years, Eric, who worked as a computer technician, stepped up his control over Margo's life. He repeatedly called her at her part-time job soon after she arrived and demanded she come home. He timed her drives home from work and checked the odometer to see if she had gone anywhere else. Eric limited their times with us to holidays and occasional visits that always ended abruptly with his temper tantrums.

Eric called Margo "dummy" and "stupid," though she carried a 4.0 grade point average in college, and "fatso" despite her tall, slender figure.

ON MISSING MARGO

Margo didn't confide much to me about her marriage, but I suspected all was not well. Our once-bubbly daughter looked sad, bewildered, and hesitant. She told me later that she had confronted Eric several times about how deeply his behavior hurt her. He only became angrier and refused to listen.

I was incensed at Eric for damaging Margo's self-esteem, and several times, I tried to speak to him without causing a scene. "Margo is my little girl," I told him. "She deserves to be treated better." He simply laughed and ignored me.

Though Margo and Eric finally sought marriage counseling, Eric refused to recognize his wrong behavior. In January 1991, Margo left him, hoping to force change, but instead her actions ignited an angry fire within him. One week after she moved out, Eric broke into her apartment, held her at knife point, and threatened to kill her and himself. My fears and anger swelled again, but I felt better the next day when Margo moved back home, obtained a restraining order, and made plans to divorce Eric. Unfortunately, she never had an opportunity to complete those plans.

Within two weeks after her death, I learned God could speak through my painful circumstances to help others like Margo. He first proved this the day Lucy Branch called from the University of Colorado at Denver, where Margo had attended college. She said the school wanted to start a free domestic violence lecture series in Margo's memory and asked if I would speak at the opening session.

I held the phone receiver, knowing I wasn't a trained speaker, but desperately wanting to do something for Margo. God impressed on me that there were other women, some trapped in battered bodies and many with bruised emotions, who needed to learn that what ultimately happened to Margo could happen to them. The lecture series would be the perfect vehicle.

On September 26, 1991, the Margo Green Lecture Series on Domestic Violence began. The speech wasn't easy to prepare. It forced me to relive emotions and reopened wounds that had not yet healed completely. Nor was the speech easy to deliver. Had I not been so nervous, I would have cried.

I addressed those women, some of whom attended with their mothers, remembering how naive our family had been. I'd learned the hard way that often girls don't trust their feelings and parents don't trust their instincts. I wanted my story to open their eyes to potential danger.

Since then, I've participated in the lecture series every year. Each time I speak, it's therapeutic. While it hurts to remember the pain, fear, and frustration of our ordeal, it helps me see the redemptive side of Margo's death: that women in dangerous relationships are being warned before their lives end in tragedy.

Once after a talk, a woman in her early twenties approached me, "I'm Jennifer," she said. "I heard you speak last year. I want you to know I got out of a bad relationship because of what you said."

I stared at her as bittersweet emotions raced through me. The hair was longer, the eyes a different color, but before me stood a triumphant "Margo," free from an abusive "Eric."

As I looked into Jennifer's eyes, I felt glad that my story had spared her Margo's fate. I reached for her hand and gave it a squeeze. "Thank you for sharing that with me," I managed to murmur. I smiled wistfully, gratified that even through the pain of my loss, Margo's life had made a difference. For that I am grateful.

Dear Lord, may I never be so focused on my own pain that I forget others need me. For I've discovered that as I reach out to ease the pain of others, my own pain is eased as well. Thank You. Amen.

The Gift

Linda Evans Shepherd

Those who hope in the LORD will renew their strength. They will soar on wings like eagles; they will run and not grow weary, they will walk and not be faint.

Isaiah 40:31

I sat in the stillness of my twenty-month-old daughter's hospital room, holding her hand, watching for signs of life. As I studied her, Laura looked as if her dark lashes would flutter open and she would sit up, ending our almost two-month-long nightmare. How I longed to hear Laura's giggle as she snuggled with her silky hair against my cheek while I read to her from one of her favorite books.

Impulsively, I leaned over and kissed her cherubic face. "Honey, it's Mommy. I love you. I know you're in there. I'm waiting."

The words caught in my throat. I shut my eyes. If only I could turn back the hand of time and avoid the collision that had saturated our lives with grief.

I remembered sitting in the emergency waiting room with my husband, tearfully waiting for the doctor's verdict. Paul and I hugged each other and shouted with joy when the doctor told us, "Laura's going to be all right; go home and get some rest." But as I lay my head on my pillow, my dreams spun out of control. I woke up in a cold sweat, picturing the blood that had trickled out of Laura's ear. *Laura is not okay. The crash was too violent. I have to get back to the hospital!*

I raced through the rain-slick, predawn streets. Once in Laura's ICU room, I found the staff gathered around her body as it quaked with convulsions.

God, where are You? I cried like David, the psalmist.

Three months later, Laura had been moved to another hospital, yet she remained unresponsive. I continued to cry, *Lord, when will You answer our prayers?*

One evening as I sat by her bed, the mechanical breathing of her respirator jarred my thoughts. A strange mood of uncertainty settled over me. I looked at the child I had fought and prayed so hard to keep. *She's really in there, isn't she?*

I stood up, trying to shake the doubt that had suddenly caught me off guard. Noticing my watch read 11:00 P.M., I began to get ready for bed. Paul was still out of town, so I had decided to sleep there in Laura's room.

The nurses had already completed their evening rounds, so I flipped off the lights and shut the door. It would be hours before anyone would check on us. I felt alone, too alone. I popped two extra-strength pain relievers and set the bottle on a nearby tray table beside my glass of water. *What if the doctors are right and Laura never wakes up?* I thought as I spread a blanket in the window seat. Fluffing my pillow, I wondered about God, *Maybe He's abandoned us. Maybe He isn't going to answer my prayers.*

This new thought punctured my tired spirit. *Just who am I trying to fool?* I questioned. *I need to face facts. Laura will never awaken. She'll live the rest of her life as a vegetable, hooked to life support.*

I tried to stifle the emotions that began to boil as Laura's respirator mocked, "no-hope, no-hope, no-hope." My chest constricted as I gasped for air. Everything seemed so different, so pointless. Laura, I decided, would be better off dead than in some suspended state of life. How could we allow our precious daughter to live out her days in that condition?

THE GIFT

〜

A plan rose from my grief. I couldn't bare to ask the doctors to take my child off life support after I had already prevented this action once before. But now, I realized Laura's smile would never return. My dreams for her life were dashed. And God? He had been as silent as Laura's stilled voice.

I was truly alone; miles from my husband, miles from Laura's cognizance, and light years from the God I had trusted. Perhaps God's silence meant I needed to take matters into my own hands. Perhaps it was up to me to end her horrible suffering.

I can kill Laura without the doctor's help, I reasoned. *I can turn off the alarms and unplug the vent from the wall. It would be so simple, except,* I wondered, *if I kill my daughter, how can I live with myself? How can I face Paul or my parents?*

The moonlight reflected on my bottle of painkillers. If I swallowed them, no one would find us until morning. Laura and I could escape this living hell together.

Just as my plan seemed like the only solution, I found my hand resting on my belly. My hidden child was only two weeks old, but I knew he was there.

My thoughts slowly cleared. *How can I kill myself? How can I kill Laura? A new life is growing inside me. A life that has the right to live!*

As my reasoning returned, I whispered a prayer. "Lord, I'm willing to wait on You, no matter the pain and the cost." The word, "wait" jolted Isaiah 40:31 into my consciousness, *They that wait upon the LORD shall renew their strength; they shall mount up with wings as eagles; they shall run, and not be weary; and they shall walk, and not faint.* (KJV)

I cried myself to sleep, terrified of the future, terrified of the murders I had almost committed.

Nine months later, my daughter began to emerge from her coma just before her baby brother, Jimmy, was born.

Although her eyes fluttered open, her gaze was fixed, she remained hooked to life support, and she slumped in her wheelchair, totally paralyzed. We were told that Laura was blind, but she began to greet us with a cheerful, "Hi!" And slowly, her eyes began to focus once again.

And although I still sometimes weep over the Laura I have lost, I embrace the Laura who has returned. How glad I am that I waited on God instead of going through with my murderous midnight plan. I still face obstacles. But God enables me to run the race set before me—a race I now know I can finish.

Dear Lord, give me strength to not merely walk through life but to run victoriously. Guide me through every obstacle. Renew my faith and my strength. Thank You for the victory I will find at the end of my race. Together, we will champion over life and death. Amen.

Endnotes

"Blue Hen Party" by Becky Freeman and "When Gifts Have Wings" by Susan Duke were taken from *Eggstra Courage for the Chicken Hearted*. Copyright © 1999 by Becky Freeman, Susan Duke, Rebecca Barlow Jordan, Gracie Malone, Fran Caffey Sandin. Published by Honor Books 1999.

"I'm Thankful for What We Still Have" was adapted from *Will I Ever Be Whole Again?* by Sandra P. Aldrich, Howard Publishing, 1999.

"Mid-Hen Crisis" by Becky Freeman was taken from *Courage for the Chicken Hearted*. Copyright © 1998 by Becky Freeman, Susan Duke, Rebecca Barlow Jordan, Gracie Malone, Fran Caffey Sandin. Published by Honor Books.

"Mother's Last Date" adapted from *Club Sandwich* by Jess Moody. Published by Broadman and Holman,. Copyright © 1999. Used by permission.

"Polliwogs in the Straining Cloth" was taken from *The Adventures of Mighty Mom*. Copyright © 2000 by Gwendolyn Mitchell Diaz. Published by Honor Books.

"Short(s) Circuited" and "Bouquet" were taken from *Normal is Just a Setting on Your Dryer* by Patsy Clairmont, a Focus on the Family book published by Tyndale House. Copyright © 1993 by Patsy Clairmont. All rights reserved. International copyright secured. Used by permission.

"They're Mothering Me to Death" by Eileen Herbert Jordan was reprinted by permission from HEALTH, C 1993.

"Tell Maggie I Love Her" as told to Robert Fulghum was taken from *True Love: Stories Told to and by Robert Fulghum*. Copyright © 1997 by Robert Fulghum. Reprinted by permission of Harper Collins Publishers, Inc.

About the Compiler

Linda Evans Shepherd, the 1997 Colorado Christian Author of the Year, has written or compiled ten books and is a member of the National Speakers Association and the Christian Leaders and Speakers Seminar (CLASS). Her one-minute radio segment, *Right to the Heart*™ is heard around the country. She conducts women's retreats and makes her audiences laugh and cry as she shares her own stories, reminding us how to be *Grumpy No More* as we *Change Our Mood and Tune Our Tudes,* and pointing out that *God Wants Spiritual Fruit Not Religious Nuts.* She also teaches *How to Make Time* for friends, family, and a relationship with God. Linda has been married for more than twenty years and has two children.

Linda may be available for your next retreat or special event. To check Linda's availability and fees, go online to http://www.sheppro.com or call 1-800-755-7007. To hear a sample of her radio show, log on to righttotheheart.com

Do you have a story for women and/or moms about friendship or Christmas to tell for a future book? If so, please send it to Linda at:

Teatime
Attn: Linda Evans Shepherd
P.O. Box 6421
Longmont, Colorado 80501
Or, e-mail (paste into the text of your e-mail to Linda at): Lswrites@aol.com (We do not accept attached files.) For editorial guidelines, please check Linda's web page at: http://www.sheppro.com or send a self-addressed, stamped envelope to the address listed above.

About the Authors

Sandra Picklesimer Aldrich, former senior editor of *Focus on the Family* magazine, is currently president and CEO of Bold Words, Inc. of Colorado Springs.

Sandy Austin lives in Lakewood, Colorado. She is a counselor at Lakewood High School and has worked in education for fourteen years. Contact Sandy at austin@worldnet.att.net

Vickie Baker's new book, *On Wings of Joy: Reflections of a Quadriplegic Trapeze Artist,* is available from her. *Surprised by Hope* is a March 2000 release.

Dr. Jeanette Blanc is a writer, college instructor, and certified counselor. She is currently enjoying a simpler, yet joyful life at home with her family.

Barbara Loftus Boswell and her husband, Brian, live in Aston, Pennsylvania, with their three children. A full-time homemaker, Barb is also a part-time nurse and freelance writer. As follow-up to their "Irish wake engagement," Barb and Brian honeymooned in Ireland!

Debbie Brockett writes for a regional magazine, *The Testimony,* and is a cofounder of Western Slope Christian Writers Association. She resides in Colorado.

Sue Cameron loves to communicate Jesus' love through words, dance, drama, and speaking. She and her husband have four children and one daughter-in-law. Ephesians 2:10 is her life verse.

Nancy Carter contributes frequently, writing short stories for a monthly feature of the *Saint Joseph News Press* and was co-editor of a family anthology.

Patsy Clairmont, humorist and best-selling author, wrote the best-selling book, *Normal Is Just a Setting on Your Dryer.* She is a favorite guest on *Focus on the Family* and speaks around the country with the Women of Faith conference.

Jan Coleman's credits include Christian magazines and *Chicken Soup* books. Her first novel reveals a deep friendship like hers and Jeanne's. E-mail her at jwriter@foothill.net

Gwendolyn Mitchell Diaz spent the first nine years of her life in Nigeria, West Africa, as a "missionary kid." She has written a weekly newspaper column focusing on family issues and feature articles for several magazines. Her book *The Adventures of Mighty Mom* was released in 2000.

Betsy Dill's inspirational and humorous articles have appeared in newspapers and magazines. She also illustrates children's books. Her latest—*Monsters in Your Bed . . . Monsters in Your Head*—addresses common childhood anxieties.

LaMarilys W. Doering was born, reared, and schooled in California. She is now a proud grandmother residing in Texas, where she serves as caregiver for her ninety-two-year-old mother. For her, writing is a spiritual journey and mission.

Rosey Dow is a missionary in Grenada, West Indies, and is the author of four romantic mysteries. She was a Reader's Favorite in 1997. Her website: http//www.angelfire.com/de/roseydow/

Maureen Dreman is a freelance writer who specializes in writing on dolls and doll collecting. In her free time, she captures life's precious moments through her essays and fiction.

Christine E. Drews was awarded Loyola College's Carroll English medal upon graduating Summa Cum Laude in 1984 with her degree in English literature. She now writes from Boulder, Colorado.

Susan Duke, best-selling author of eight books and inspirational speaker and singer, resides with her husband in East Texas. She is one of the Hens With Pens, authors of *Courage for the Chicken Hearted* and *Eggstra Courage for the Chicken Hearted.* Speaking information: (903) 883-3355 or e-mail: suzieduke@juno.com

Marjorie Evans, a former elementary school teacher, is now a freelance writer. She and her husband, Edgar, live in California with their Welsh Corgi.

Becky Freeman is a national speaker and author of several best-selling books on family humor. Drop by to visit her "front porch" at www.beckyfreeman.com

Cynthia Fronk, is owner and president of a national health & safety consulting and training company. Cindy lives on a Colorado ranch with her husband, John. Together they raise Alpacas and Appaloosa horses.

Robert Fulghum is the best-selling author of *All I Really Need to Know I Learned in Kindergarten.* His story, "Tell Maggie I Love Her," is from his book *True Love: Stories Told to and by Robert Fulghum.*

Rudy Galdonik is a professional speaker, open-heart surgery patient, and widow. She uses passion and humor to encourage audiences to turn today's challenges into tomorrow's credentials.

Verda J. Glick is a missionary in El Salvador. Her book, *Deliver the Ransom Alone,* tells about her husband's kidnapping. Part of that story appeared in *Guidepost.* E-mail: glorias@vianet.com.sv

Cindy Heflin enjoys writing, reading, and traveling with her family. Encouraging women to seek God and trust Him unconditionally is her passion. She and her husband, Bryant, have two daughters. E-mail: heflin.1976@prodigy.net

Nancy Hoag, author of *Good Morning! Isn't It a Fabulous Day!* and *Storms Pass, So Hang On!,* has won numerous writing awards, including First Place/Christian Reader 1998 and Third Place/Writer's Digest 1999.

Mary van Balen Holt is an author, educational consultant, and writes a monthly column on experiencing God in everyday life. Her books include: *A Dwelling Place Within, All Earth Is Crammed with Heaven: Daily Reflections for Mothers,* and *Marriage: A Covenant of Seasons.* E-mail: vbholt@computech-online.net

Nancy Kennedy lives in Inverness, Florida, with her husband, Barry, and youngest daughter, Laura. She loves her job as the religion reporter of her local newspaper and editor of a monthly magazine for senior citizens. Her latest book is *Prayers God Always Answers* (WaterBrook Press).

Cheryl Kirking is a popular women's conference speaker, songwriter, and author. Contact her at P.O. Box 525, Lake Mills, Wisconsin 53551. Tel: (920) 648-8959; ckirking@gdinet.com.

Sherri Langton is associate editor of the *Bible Advocate* magazine, as well as a freelance writer and workshop speaker.

Patricia Lorenz is an inspirational writer and speaker who drinks tea every day in her home in Oak Creek, Wisconsin. For speaking engagements, contact Associated Speakers Inc. at 1-800-437-7577.

Kelly J. Martindale, author and speaker, lives with her family in Colorado. Her articles range from parenting and women's issues to travel and horses and are found in national publications. E-mail: kellyjfm@oneimage.com.

Kathy Collard Miller is a popular speaker and best-selling author of forty books including *Through His Eyes.* E-mail: http://www.larryandkathy.com.

Jess Moody is a professional storyteller and public speaker. For many years, he pastored Shepherd of the Hills Church in Porter Ranch, California. He lives with his wife, Doris, in Mansfield, Texas.

Lynda Munfrada lives in Colorado with her husband of twenty years and three beautiful children. She praises God for her Christian family and for His continual grace, love, and laughter!

Susan Titus Osborn is director of the TCC Manuscript Critique Service and a contributing editor of *The Christian Communicator* magazine. She has authored twenty-one books and numerous articles. Contact Susan at: 3133 Puente Street, Fullerton, California 92835; (714) 990-1532; Susanosb@aol.com; web site: christiancommunicator.com

Deborah Raney is an award-winning novelist whose first book, *A Vow to Cherish,* inspired World Wide Pictures' film of the same title. Deborah and her husband have four children and make their home in Kansas.

Naomi Rhode, CSP, CPAE Speaker's Hall of Fame, past president of National Speaker's Association, and 1997 winner of the Cavett Award is author of two books. She is also coauthor and contributor for numerous books and publications.

Heidi Hess Saxton is senior editor at Servant Publications and a freelance writer.

Sheila Seifert is a full-time freelance writer residing in Colorado.

Mary Kay Shelby lives with her husband, Derek, and their four children on a small farm outside Charlotte, North Carolina, where they are learning the art and wisdom of country living.

Carolyn Standerfer is an inspirational writer, leader of relational recovery groups, wife, mother, and home school teacher. Contact her at carolyns@hughes.net or (661) 722-9146.

Le Ann Thieman is an author and professional speaker. She motivates audiences to balance their lives, truly live their priorities, and make a difference in the world. She can be reached at 1-877-THIEMAN.

Carol J. Van Drie is a forty-two-year-old army wife and writer. She has been married twenty-plus years and has three children.

Connie Bertelsen Young is a freelance writer and has written the column "Valley Gal" for two California newspapers for seven years. Contact: valegal@juno.com.

Additional copies of this book
are available from your local bookstore.

If you have enjoyed this book,
or if it has impacted your life,
we would like to hear from you.

Please contact us at:

Honor Books
Department E
P.O. Box 55388
Tulsa, Oklahoma 74155
Or by e-mail at info@honorbooks.com